Special Report

MACHINE VISION SYSTEMS

Tech Tran Consultants, Inc.

Lake Geneva, Wisconsin

SECOND EDITION

McGRAW-HILL BOOK COMPANY

New York   St. Louis   San Francisco   Auckland   Bogotá
Hamburg   Johannesburg   London   Madrid   Mexico   Montreal
New Delhi   Panama   Paris   São Paulo   Singapore
Sydney   Tokyo   Toronto

Library of Congress Cataloging-in-Publication Data
Main entry under title:
Machine vision systems / Tech Tran Consultants, Inc.
   (A Tech Tran special report)
   1. Computer vision.   I. Tech Tran Consultants.
II. Series.
TA1632.M34   1985   006.3'7   85-23748
ISBN 0-07-063243-X

1234567890   EDW/EDW   89876

Printed and bound by Edwards Brothers.

CONTENTS

FOREWORD

Machine vision has emerged as one of the most important new
technologies for the factory of the future, as well as the factory of
today. If properly applied, machine vision can dramatically reduce
production costs and improve product quality by enabling accurate and
inexpensive 100% inspection of workpieces. Its non-contacting nature
also means that machine vision will become an important sensor for
determining workpiece identification, position, orientation, shape
and other characteristics in future robotic and flexible
manufacturing systems. Regardless of the products involved, almost
every manufacturing organization should be considering the use of
machine vision in its own operations.

In response to this interest, over 100 companies now offer industrial
machine vision systems for use in assembly, inspection, and other
manufacturing operations. From little more than a laboratory
research instrument during the 1970's, machine vision has become a
useful manufacturing tool and has led to the development of a new
industry. Although a great deal has occurred in this field during
the past five years, many developments are still happening at a rapid
pace. Machine vision has yet to become a widely used tool.

What is the present state-of-the-art of the machine vision industry,
current technology, and applications? And what is the future outlook
for the technology and the industry? This report was prepared to
answer these questions and provide an assessment of the machine
vision field, including a review of current and future technology,
industrial applications and industry structure.

This report has been written for manufacturing managers, engineers,
marketing managers, strategic planners, entrepreneurs, and anyone
else who needs to quickly be brought up to date on this exciting new

industry. It is not intended to be a technical manual, nor is it intended to be a market research study. Written in a business oriented style, the report is intended to provide business and technical specialists with a balanced overview and a single source of information on current technology, applications, commercial systems, opportunities, and future trends in the machine vision system field.

This second edition of the report represents a completely revised and expanded version of a report originally published in 1983. It contains data on over 120 systems manufactured by nearly 90 vendors, over four times the number contained in the original report. The second edition also presents the results of a survey of machine vision suppliers concerning current and future markets and likely technological developments.

The report begins with an introduction to the basic concepts of image interpretation in Chapter 1. This includes a discussion of the process of image formation, the various ways in which images can be described, and the process of human perception and image interpretation.

Chapter 2 consists of a discussion of the fundamental concepts of machine vision. Included here is a definition of machine vision, a discussion of the basic functions of machine vision, an examination of the machine vision process including components of machine vision systems, and a review of criteria by which machine vision performance can be evaluated.

In Chapter 3, suitable machine vision applications are reviewed. Criteria for determining the feasibility of machine vision in a particular application are outlined, machine vision capabilities are compared with those of humans, and specific applications are discussed.

Chapter 4 reviews the specifications of commercially available machine vision systems. Profiles of leading suppliers are presented, and an assessment is made of current vision system limitations and developmental needs.

Chapter 5 reviews current developmental efforts taking place in industry, government, and private research organizations. A forecast of likely future developments in vision system technology, applications, and industry structure is presented. Included here are market forecasts for the next ten years.

Three appendices provide a list of organizations involved in the machine vision field, a recommended list of published information sources, and a glossary of machine vision terms.

This special report is one of several published by Tech Tran on significant, new, manufacturing-related technologies. Tech Tran is a consulting and publishing firm focusing on advanced production processes and equipment. Tech Tran also publishes Manufacturing Technology Horizons™, a newsletter on new developments. Other Tech Tran divisions include The Manufacturing Technology Bookstore™ and Manufacturing Technology Press™.

CHAPTER 1
INTRODUCTION TO VISUAL PERCEPTION

The concept of machine vision began more than 20 years ago. Initially, the field was almost exclusively the domain of academic researchers. However, in the mid-1960's, experiments in electronic image processing techniques began to capture the interest of a number of possible users, particularly for such applications as military reconnaissance, satellite image processing, medical testing and optical character recognition. It was not until the late-1970's that shop floor applications of machine vision began to be a practical reality.

Many individuals within the industry and research community consider machine vision to be a subset of the larger field of artificial intelligence, particularly with regard to computer perception. Others view machine vision as a separate topic based on a number of other fields, such as image processing, pattern recognition and scene analysis. In either case, machine vision represents a relatively complex subject drawing upon many technical disciplines.

In order to better understand machine vision, it is helpful to first consider the more general subject of visual perception. Comparisons to the human eye/brain system are also useful in developing a better insight into how objects are sensed and recognized by machines.

Vision sensing is a form of non-contact sensing, and so the recognition process does not deal directly with the objects under consideration. Instead, a representation of the scene must be created in the form of an image. Next, the various features of this image, such as location, shape, and orientation, are described and measured. Finally, these measurements are compared with various models of expected results to infer the true nature of the original object or set of objects from which the image was formed. These three steps, which are discussed in the following sections, form the basis for the process known as machine vision.

IMAGE FORMATION

An image is a two-dimensional representation of a scene. A scene is a two or three-dimensional object or group of objects arranged in a random or orderly configuration. An image can either be analog, such as that formed by the human eye, or it may be digital, such as the N x M array of discrete picture elements formed by machine vision systems for computer processing. Even the simplest image that we normally encounter contains an enormous amount of information. The mechanism by which the human eye is able to process and accurately interpret a complex image is so advanced that it is not yet completely understood. However, the principles of image formation are much better known.

Whether an image is analog or digital, the ability to form an image is based upon the fundamental law of physics that all matter emits electromagnetic radiation, which is either internally generated or reflected by an object from some energy source. This energy is generated in the form of a wave, which can be characterized by an amplitude and a frequency. In the visible light range, amplitude determines the intensity of the light received from a certain point on an object, while frequency determines the color. Every image therefore consists of a pattern of varying light intensities and, in some cases, varying colors.

In a non-colored image, such as a black and white photograph, it is the variations in light intensities that allows us to interpret the image as representing a specific scene, for example, a three-dimensional object or group of objects. An entire scene is reproduced in an image as a collection of various shades of gray. The boundaries between different shades may be sharply defined, with abrupt changes in intensity, or they may be seen as gradual changes in intensities. The specific level of intensity which is observed at a particular point on the image is a function of four scene-related variables: the source of illumination for the scene, the reflectivity of the surface of an object at that point, the orientation of the surface, and the nature of the sensor which receives light from the scene.

Illumination

In a manufacturing environment in which some form of manual or automated visual inspection is being performed, workpieces are examined by observing the characteristics of light which is reflected from each workpiece. This light originates from a source of illumination, such as a lamp directed toward the production line. In addition to a lamp, there would normally be a secondary source of illumination from ambient lighting in the plant. The light from the lamp may be reflected from other equipment back to the workpiece to provide another weak secondary source of light. Another complicating factor is the diffusion of light, which causes a dimmer surface at greater distances. The result is a complicated pattern of illumination striking the workpiece.

Another complicating factor is the fact that artificial light sources are generally not uniform in intensity. The ideal light source would be a single point located at an infinite distance, which is approximated by the sun. In a manufacturing environment, however, a lamp or spotlight may provide varying light intensities at different points along the surface of a workpiece. This can affect the nature of shadows and shadings on the surface, which can affect the interpretation of the object.

Reflectivity

The ability of an object to reflect all or a portion of the light incident upon its surface is determined by such surface characteristics as texture or color. An object of uniform color and smoothness would reflect light uniformly from all points on its surface. Real objects, however, have varying surface characteristics, and so varying degrees of brightness are observed on images. Darker colors reflect less light than lighter colors, and rougher surfaces tend to diffuse light more than smooth surfaces, resulting in less reflected light.

Surface Orientation

Variations in light intensity may also be a result of the geometry of the surface of an object. A surface which is perpendicular to the path of a light beam will appear brighter than that which is aligned at some other angle. Thus, in the image of the cube shown in Exhibit 1, the surface which is most nearly perpendicular to the path of the light beam appears brightest, while the others are correspondingly darker.

In the case of curved surfaces, as in the cylinder, the change from one shade to another is not abrupt as in the cube. Instead, there is a continuous change in intensity as the surface orientation gradually changes. Objects with more complex geometries, such as a plastic fluid bottle with a handle, will show complex variations in surface brightness in the image. In this example, the handle may act as an

EXHIBIT 1

EFFECTS OF SURFACE ORIENTATION ON IMAGE LIGHT INTENSITY

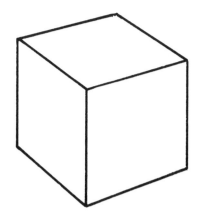

(a) CUBE AND CYLINDER WITH UNIFORM LIGHTING

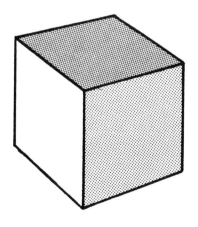

LIGHT SOURCE

(b) CUBE AND CYLINDER WITH LIGHT SOURCE AT LEFT

occlusion, which would prevent light from reaching the surface of the bottle. The result of an occlusion is a shadow, or region of significantly lower intensity, on the surface.

Sensor Characteristics

The final variable affecting the level of intensity at any point on an image is the response pattern of the sensor which detects the light from the object. The human eye, for example, does not perceive light in a precisely uniform manner over the entire retina. Further, the eye tends to over or underestimate the level of intensity of an image under varying conditions, such as in situations when relative contrasts are exceptionally high or low. Also, the eye tends to become fatigued over time, so that estimates of relative intensities tend to vary over time. Although mechanical sensors are less subject to these variations, there still are certain definable variations in response which may be present over the surface of the sensor.

IMAGE FEATURES

The four variables discussed above have an impact on the way in which light is reflected from various objects within a scene and detected by a sensor. The resulting distribution of light intensities forms an image, which is a two-dimensional representation of a scene. This image can then be analyzed to infer the true nature of the object or group of objects which are represented by the image.

An image of an object can be described in terms of a number of visual characteristics, or "features". These features can be categorized into three groups: those that represent the object's position in space, those that describe the geometry or shape of the object, and those that describe the distribution of light intensity over the surface of the object.

Position

An object at any given time is at a specific location in space, it is oriented in a specific direction, and it may be moving in a certain way. The determination of these features represents the most basic level of object identification. In order to fully define an object's position, three basic features must be determined: the object's location, its orientation, and its motion.

Location

The location of an object refers to its coordinates in space. Since an object occupies a finite volume of space, its coordinates are typically defined relative to a specific point on the object. A correct physical interpretation of location would require the determination of the center of mass or center of gravity. However, in vision sensing, an object is represented by a two-dimensional image, and therefore the centroid (i.e., center of gravity for the two-dimensional image) is normally used as a reference point. Two pieces of information are generally required. First, the distance of the object (at some point on the surface) from the observer must be measured. Secondly, the direction of the object relative to some reference line must be determined. In a simple visual inspection situation on a production line, all objects may pass through a specified field of view at a constant distance from the observer, and so direction can be measured by determining the horizontal and vertical position of each object within the field of view. In this case, it is not necessary to measure distance.

Orientation

An object may be oriented in many different ways without changing its location. Orientation refers to the direction of a specified axis of the object. A simplified approach to specifying orientation is to calculate the axis of least moment of inertia of the image. This is a mathematically determined axis around which, if the object were spinning, it would offer less resistance to a change in motion than around any other axis. Intuitively, this is the "lengthwise" axis of a long object. In Exhibit 2(a), these axes are shown for a batch of wrenches randomly arranged on a conveyor belt. The orientation angles are shown relative to a horizontal reference line. The problem becomes more difficult in Exhibit 2(b), which shows a top view of several dice. The axis of least moment of inertia can be along either of two diagonals of the square image. Further, in the case of the two dice with sixes on the top surface, the diagonal axes do not indicate that one die is oriented 90° from the other. Finally, in viewing the eight-balls of Exhibit 2(c), no information about orientation is available without analyzing surface markings.

Motion

A scene may change over time as a result of the motion of objects. There are certain factory situations, such as in the avoidance of collisions, when it is useful to determine the speed of an object along with its direction of motion (i.e., its velocity). Motion results in a change of location or orientation over time. The human eye is remarkably proficient at judging motions, while machine vision systems are extremely primitive in this area.

Geometric Configuration

EXHIBIT 2

DETERMINATION OF ORIENTATION OF OBJECTS

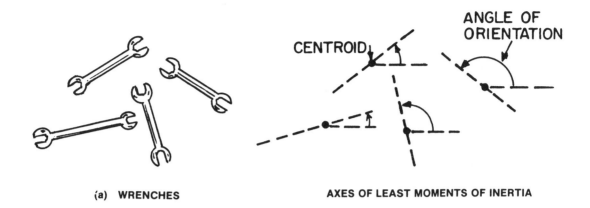

(a) WRENCHES   AXES OF LEAST MOMENTS OF INERTIA

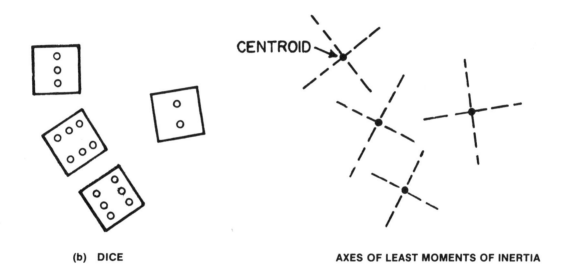

(b) DICE   AXES OF LEAST MOMENTS OF INERTIA

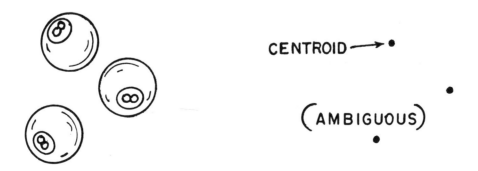

(c) EIGHT BALLS   AXES OF LEAST MOMENTS OF INERTIA

The determination of the position of an object or group of objects will provide only the most elementary information about the possible identity of an image. An additional level of understanding can be achieved by analyzing the geometrical configuration of an image. An image is made up of a series of regions, which are areas of (approximately) constant light intensity. Boundaries between regions of different intensities may result from discontinuities in the geometry of an object, changes in surface characteristics, or shadings caused by external sources of illumination. In an idealized situation, these boundaries would all be sharply defined lines. In reality, there are also many situations in which regions gradually change in intensity over an area until they merge into other regions. The goal here is to identify those basic geometric features which can be determined by analyzing regions which have sharply defined boundaries. This includes three types of features, as discussed below.

Boundary Locations

Image segmentation is the process of breaking an image into a series of well defined segments or regions, each separated by a well defined boundary. The identification of all major image boundaries results in the creation of a line drawing as a representation of the image. In many real-world manufacturing situations, such a simple silhouette pattern of an image is adequate to accurately identify workpieces which have clearly recognizable outlines. In cases where simple outside silhouettes are not adequate for a positive identification, additional image boundaries within the image can be analyzed. An image boundary may represent the true edge of a surface (on a cube, for example), it may represent an apparent edge at a point where the line of sight becomes tangent to the surface, it may represent a sudden surface discontinuity (such as a change in color or textures), or it may represent a discontinuity caused by illumination, such as a shadow. Based upon a prior model of expected three-dimensional configurations of an object, along with knowledge of illumination

10

characteristics, it may be possible to interpret these boundaries.

Shapes

Each region of the image that has been defined by an enclosed set of
boundaries can be characterized according to several geometric
features, all relating to the shape of the regions. If the image is
a simple object, perhaps it can be described as a simple geometric
form, such as a square or a triangle. In certain cases, this may
provide useful information about the assumed three-dimensional shape
of an object. For example, a parallelogram in certain configurations
could be assumed to be an image of one side of a cube as seen from an
angle. For more complex images, additional features can be
calculated, such as surface area, centroid location, boundary
perimeter, or specific boundary dimensions. In many manufacturing
situations, workpieces are designed with well-defined geometric
profiles, which can easily be compared with actual line images to
insure quality control.

Image Organization

Once all sharply defined image boundaries have been identified and
shapes have been determined, additional information can be gathered
by analyzing the way in which the image regions are arranged relative
to each other. If a cube is viewed toward a vertical edge from a
point above the horizontal surface upon which it rests, the image
formed will be a set of three connected parallelograms. The shape of
these figures, along with the way in which they border each other,
implies that they represent the surfaces of a cube, one being the top
and the other two being sides. An image, or pattern of light
intensities, can be thought of as a hierarchy of individual segments,
or "primitives". One method of representing an image is to create a
hierarchical structure which logically represents the way the
components of the image are interconnected. In this "syntactic" view

of patterns, an image is shown as a tree, a string, or a block diagram of all basic components of the image.

Exhibit 3 shows how several different objects might be represented in a hierarchical manner. The cube in Exhibit 3(a) consists of three elements, a top and two sides. Each surface is shown in the block diagram not only to be a part of the cube, but also to have certain relationships with each other. For example, side A is below top C and also to the left of side B. In Exhibit 3(b), a more complex scene, consisting of two objects, is depicted in the block diagram. The column consists of two cylinders, which are presented by the visible surfaces D, E, and F. Exhibit 3(c) shows how the letter "A" might be represented. Starting from the top, three different types of lines (1, 2, and 3) are joined in a specific pattern to form the letter. Other letters would consist of different lines, and they would be joined in different patterns.

These examples show that an image can be viewed in two different contexts. First, an image is formed globally as a two-dimensional representation of a complete scene (e.g., a "cube" or a "cube and column"). Secondly, a local view of an image considers it to be a logical pattern of individual elements (or segments, or primitives), which collectively form a two-dimensional representation of an object or group of objects.

Light Intensity Distribution

All of the features discussed to this point describe images which are essentially two-dimensional line drawings. For many of the manufacturing applications in which machine vision systems are currently used, the ability to recognize line drawings or silhouettes is sufficient. Many manufactured parts are easily identified from

EXHIBIT 3

HIERARCHICAL REPRESENTATIONS OF OBJECTS

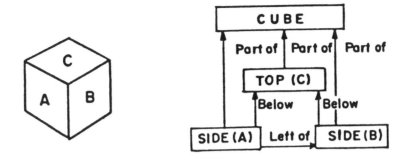

(a) 3-DIMENSIONAL CUBE

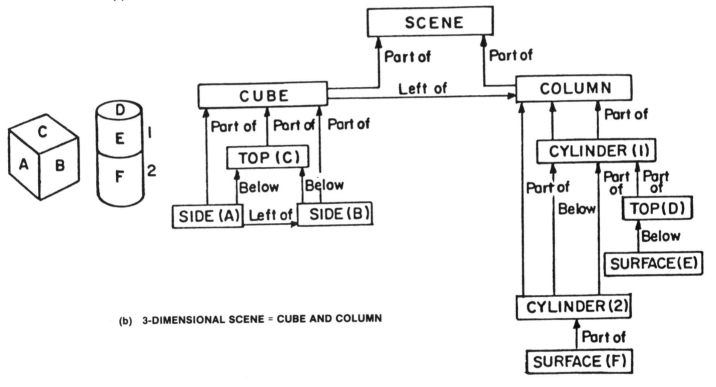

(b) 3-DIMENSIONAL SCENE = CUBE AND COLUMN

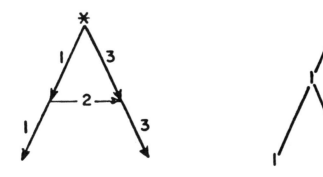

(c) 2-DIMENSIONAL LETTER "A"

simple geometrical features.

For simple manufactured parts with clearly identifiable geometries, the formation of images consisting only of image region boundaries is adequate. However, greatly increased understanding of an image is achieved when light intensity variations over surfaces can be represented in an image. As was discussed earlier, changes in light intensity may be caused by illumination factors, by sensor factors, or by surface factors such as texture or color. The sharply defined boundaries considered until now have been assumed to be caused by sudden discontinuities, such as edges. But true images consist of complex patterns of continuously varying intensities within regions. Curved surfaces, for example, produce images in which intensities gradually change from light to dark. A complete description of an image thus requires a representation of the image intensity distribution over the entire area of the image.

IMAGE INTERPRETATION

The human eye is basically a sophisticated vision sensor, in some ways similar to a TV camera. Its function is to gather and assemble raw visual data about the environment external to the body. This data is assembled in the form of a two-dimensional image of a scene. This image can be characterized according to a series of features, as described above. These features are then interpreted by the brain, which converts this raw image into useful information from which decisions can be made (e.g., the decision of which path to follow around an obstacle).

The ultimate goal of visual perception is to sense and interpret the characteristics of objects within an individual's field of view either for the purpose of making immediate decisions about the body's motions or for changing an existing set of beliefs about the environment (e.g., learning). In order to generate useful information for decision making, a correct interpretation of the image must be made. The mechanism of human perception has been the subject of intense study for the past two decades, and a complete understanding of this mechanism has not yet been achieved.

The study of human perception has, in fact, evolved into two separate but related disciplines: pattern recognition and artificial intelligence. Both areas began with the similar objective of attempting to understand the process by which humans are able to recognize objects based upon an analysis of two-dimensional images. Especially intriguing to researchers was the ability of humans to correctly identify an object without needing to know specific details of the object, such as size, position, colors, and so on. Each discipline approached this issue in different ways. Pattern recognition research concentrated on methods of constructing and interpreting images, while artificial intelligence research addressed such areas as human intelligence modelling, natural languages and human problem solving. Today, as machine vision capabilities become more sophisticated, research in pattern recognition is increasingly making use of new techniques developed in the artificial intelligence area.

General Theory of Human Perception

The remarkable aspect of the human eye/brain system is its ability to quickly interpret a complex two-dimensional image and, based upon this data, identify three-dimensional objects. In addition to identifying objects, the human system can determine several characteristics of these objects, such as texture, colors, shape, orientation, approximate dimensions, distance and even motion.

It is not entirely clear whether the human eye/brain system forms a perception of a scene by first studying the entire scene as a whole (a global approach) or by first sensing discrete components of the scene and then structuring them in the mind until the entire scene is interpreted (a local approach). Intuitively, it appears that we view an entire scene at once using parallel processing of all elements and form conclusions based upon a total impression. It could be assumed that we fill in the details of the scene only as required to identify specific elements with greater certainty. In fact, most researchers today feel that human perception combines a top-down with a bottom-up approach to image processing. The degree to which a global versus a local analysis is relied upon depends on the extent to which previous models of the scene have been developed and stored in memory. A quick overall glance at a familiar room establishes its identity, while a more detailed bottom-up analysis of individual scene elements may be required to establish the identity of an unfamiliar room.

Whichever approach is used, it appears that the human eye/brain system tends to view a scene as a hierarchy of groups and sub-groups of elements. A room consists of a structural group (walls, floor, ceiling), a surface covering group (wallpaper, carpet, drapes, etc.), a furnishing group (table, chairs, lamps, bookcases, etc.), and perhaps other major groups. Each group can be broken into several subgroups which in turn can be further segmented down to the level of a large number of very basic elements.

Another generally accepted view of human perception is that it relies heavily on the use of symbolism for interpreting images. This is made possible by the vast number of previous visual experiences which are stored in the human memory. Cartoon characters are drawn with extensive use of symbols, as are the many graphic symbols used in advertising. The poison symbol used on many toxic substance containers requires no analysis; its symbolism is immediately obvious.

Example: Perception of a Room

Consider the image one receives upon entering a room. At a minimum, a room consists of certain basic geometric elements, such as a floor, a ceiling, and walls. In its most simplified form, a room might appear as shown in Exhibit 4. This image consists of several regions and image boundaries, as discussed earlier. A region is an area of the image over which light intensity is constant. In this highly simplified example, one of the walls can be considered to be a region of constant light intensity. An image boundary is a discontinuity in the light intensity of the image, i.e., a boundary between one region and another. Any of the eight lines is an image boundary.

But how does the human eye/brain system know that this is in fact a room and not something else? This simple example is ambiguous in the sense that there are several physical models which this image can represent. First, it could be a plane with lines drawn upon it. Secondly, it could be a top view of a pyramid with the top cut off. Third, it could be the inside of a box-shaped figure, which may or may not be a room. A positive identification can only be made by removing the ambiguities.

There are two ways by which the human eye/brain system minimizes ambiguities. First, several theories of human intelligence suggest that the human brain assists in interpreting images by providing a series of preconceived notions, or models, about what to expect upon encountering a scene. These models, which are stored in the brain's memory, form the basis of all human learning. Based upon past experiences, we expect that upon entering a room we will see, at a

17

INTERPRETATION OF A
BASIC LINE IMAGE OF A ROOM

EXHIBIT 4

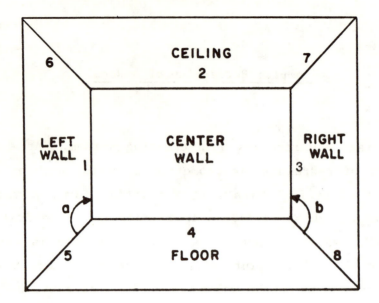

STEPS	TESTS
1. IDENTIFY LINE 4	• IS LINE 4 HORIZONTAL? • IS LINE 4 BELOW LINE OF SIGHT?
2. IDENTIFY LINE 1	• IS LINE 1 VERTICAL? • DOES LINE 1 BEGIN AT LEFT END OF LINE 4?
3. IDENTIFY LINE 3	• IS LINE 3 VERTICAL? • DOES LINE 3 BEGIN AT RIGHT END OF LINE 4?
4. IDENTIFY LINE 2	• IS LINE 2 HORIZONTAL? • IS LINE 2 ABOVE LINE OF SIGHT? • DOES LINE 2 JOIN TOP ENDS OF LINES 1 AND 3?
5. IDENTIFY LINE 5	• DOES LINE 5 BEGIN WHERE LINES 1 AND 4 JOIN? • IS DIRECTION OF LINE 5 TOWARD LOWER LEFT?
6. IDENTIFY LINES 6, 7 AND 8	• ETC.
7. MOVE TO THE RIGHT	• DOES ANGLE a DECREASE? • DOES ANGLE b INCREASE?

minimum, four walls along with a ceiling and a floor. If the room is familiar, we may also expect to see many other features, such as a carpet, windows, and a variety of furniture. These models enable us to make assumptions about the nature of objects within our field of view without the need for a detailed analysis of the image. Even when the image is ambiguous and can be interpreted in more than one way, our models of reality allow us to quickly decide which alternative interpretation is most likely to be correct.

A second way in which ambiguities are minimized is to generate direct information through the process of image interpretation. In the simplified example of Exhibit 4, we only have certain basic geometrical landmarks to assist in determining the identity of the image. In order to decide which of the three possible shapes this image represents, a series of hypotheses is required. For example, we might assume that line 4 (the floor/center wall edge) must be horizontal and located below eye level if this is a normal room. Further, moving left and right along this edge, we might expect to encounter the vertical lines 1 and 3 at the corners. Similar assumptions could be made about all other edges until the shape shown in Exhibit 4 is determined.

The location and orientation of these surfaces is not yet determined, however. A method of determining distances to the surfaces is required. This is accomplished in two ways by the human eye/brain system. First, the use of two eyes is a means of measuring parallax, or the apparent displacement of an object relative to another object when viewed from two different points. Secondly, by simply moving from one point to another in the room, each surface appears to distort, with the amount of distortion directly related to the orientation of the surface and the amount which the observer moves. For example, in step 7 of the identification process in Exhibit 4, a simple test is to observe whether the angles a and b increase or decrease as we move to the right. If angle a decreases, it can be assumed that the left surface comes out from the center wall toward the observer (a decrease implies that the surface is oriented away from the observer).

The result of this process indicates that the image is that of the inside of a box-shaped figure. But is it truly a room? And what kind of a room is it? Moving to a more complex image, we assume that the room is a normally furnished office. A simple image of such a room consisting of lines (boundaries) and areas within the lines (regions) would be more complex, resulting in more data from which conclusions could be drawn. Again, we call upon a series of stored models which provide reference frames for evaluating the nature of the room. There are general models for various categories of rooms, such as living rooms, offices, and kitchens. There are also models for components of rooms, such as types of walls, floor coverings, or furnishings. As we enter the room, the assumptions of these models are systematically tested against the observed characteristics of the image until the best fit is determined. In this example, we would conclude that the room is an office, based upon the presence of such image shapes as:

- An object which matches our preconceived model of an office desk.

- A rectangular shaped object which matches our model of a file cabinet.

- An object shaped like an office chair.

Until now, the image has been defined by a series of regions and image boundaries (or edges in three-dimensional space). An additional level of refinement could be achieved by adding surface details to the objects in the room, such as surface light intensity variations. In this case, a "real-world" image would be produced, consisting of textures, varying surface orientations, and shadows. Each object in the room can be identified not just from its boundary configurations, but from an analysis of subtle changes in shading over surfaces areas, for example. Metal handles and trim appear lighter than other items, adding further evidence to support the assumed identity of the objects. If the image were in color, one more level of refinement would be added (for example, a green color on an assumed image of a plant).

As each level of complexity is added to the image, a wealth of new data is made available to the observer. The eye/brain system is able to rapidly test each segment of the image by comparing it with the model stored in the brain's memory. The closer the image segment matches the assumed model, the greater is the likelihood that the image segment will be correctly identified.

Image Ambiguities

The goal of the image interpretation process is to reduce ambiguities in the image (i.e., the number of possible ways in which it can be interpreted) to a minimum. If preconceived models are inadequate to explain the image, then the image must be analyzed further, moving from simple boundary determination to increasingly complex levels of differentiation within the image until enough information is available to form a conclusion.

In certain situations, ambiguities cannot be completely removed, and the human eye/brain system is unable to make a definite interpretation of an image. The most common example of this is the optical illusion. In the simple example shown in Exhibit 5(a), it can be assumed that the image is that of a three-dimensional figure, a cube with two intersecting planes attached. However, it is impossible to determine if the planes are attached to the top or

21

EXHIBIT 5

REDUCTION OF IMAGE AMBIGUITY THROUGH THE USE OF ILLUMINATION

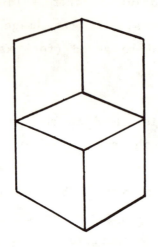

(a)   IMAGE WITH UNIFORM ILLUMINATION

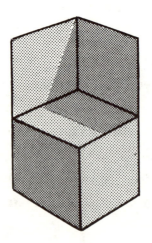

(b)   IMAGE WITH LIGHT SOURCE AT UPPER RIGHT

bottom of the cube. In this case, our information is limited to a simple determination of boundary locations. Without additional evidence, no further conclusions can be drawn. In Exhibit 5(b), that evidence is provided through the use of a source of illumination placed to the right of the object. Now a series of seven individual shaded regions can be studied. Based upon our model of how light intensity should vary under each of the two alternative explanations for this image, we can now conclude that the planes are attached to the top of the cube.

HUMAN VS. MACHINE PERCEPTION

Although the example of the human eye/brain system is useful in understanding machine vision, this analogy should not be carried too far. There are many similarities between the two processes, but there are also major differences, which are discussed later in the report.

CHAPTER 2
MACHINE VISION

Machine vision, often referred to as computer vision or intelligent vision, is a means of electro-mechanically simulating the image recognition capability of the human eye/brain system. The tremendous interest in machine vision at the present time is a result of a number of recent developments. First, the large amount of data that must be processed in order to interpret an image requires that powerful computers be available. Recent decreases in computer costs along with increases in capacity as a result of microelectronics have made these computers more feasible for use with vision systems. At the same time, advances have been made in the understanding of how image processing should be performed. This has led to the development of corresponding software algorithms which allow machine vision systems to simulate the human visual process. Finally, advances have been made in the hardware used to generate images, such as the development of solid state cameras.

DEFINITION

An intuitive notion of machine vision might be to consider it a type of sensing capability, similar to the way the human eye acts as the body's vision sensor. This would be only partially correct, however. The human eye receives light from an object and then converts this light into electrical signals. It does not interpret these signals or make decisions based upon the nature of the image. Image interpretation and decision making are performed by the brain. Only when the eye and brain are considered together is it appropriate to discuss a human vision system rather than a vision sensor.

In the same way, a machine vision system includes both a visual sensing and an interpretive capability. An imaging device, such as a vidicon camera, is nothing more than a visual sensor which receives light (through a lens) and converts it to electrical signals (through a vidicon tube). When a data processing device such as a microcomputer is employed, these signals can be refined and analyzed to allow interpretation of the scene which generated the signals. In other words, imaging alone can be thought of simply as a means of providing visual input signals to a computer for processing. The signal that is received by the computer is actually no different than the electrical signal generated through a keyboard or other input device.

Other definitions of machine vision also exist. These include: "a process of producing useful symbolic descriptions of a visual environment from image data," and "the automatic interpretation of imagery to control a manufacturing process." Unfortunately, machine vision is like the phrase "machine tool." Both are somewhat poorly defined, cover a wide range of equipment, and bring to mind a number of different interpretations based on an individual's persepctive.

The definition of a machine vision system as discussed in this report requires that at least the following three basic elements be present:

- <u>Image formation capability</u> - This is the ability to receive incoming light from an object or a scene, convert the light into electrical signals, and then process the signals until they are in a form that is compatible with computer processing capabilities. The result is a digital array of bits of data which represents an image.

- <u>Image analysis capability</u> - This is the ability to analyze and measure various characteristics of the image.

- Image interpretation capability - The third basic element required in a machine vision system is the ability to interpret the image in such a way that some useful decision can be made about the object or scene being studied. This is provided by a computer.

This definition of machine vision makes a clear distinction between several broad categories of optical sensing equipment currently used in manufacturing applications. The definition eliminates, for example, such equipment as optical comparators which are used to project silhouettes of a workpiece onto a viewing screen. Such systems do not possess the image analysis and interpretation capability normally associated with a machine vision system. Similarly, the definition excludes equipment such as photocells and other light-beam equipment for measuring presence or dimensions, and closed-circuit television systems used by human operators for off-line inspection applications.

BASIC FUNCTIONS

Like the human eye/brain system, a machine vision system can be used to interpret an image for one of two general reasons: to cause some immediate decision to be made during a production operation (e.g., avoid a collision, move a part to a correct orientation relative to another part, or reject a defective part), or to build a data base about a series of workpieces so that some analytical model can be developed to describe the expected characteristics of the objects (i.e., for learning). Simple models are being used in production applications primarily for making decisions during inspection or processing operations. In some applications, data bases are being maintained for such purposes as inventory monitoring.

This ability to automatically sense a situation (object or scene), interpret the resulting data, and then make some decision based upon the findings provides machine vision systems with a remarkable degree of flexibility. To accomplish this end, vision systems are designed to perform three general functions: verify the presence or absence of an object, measure image features, and recognize objects. The features which vision systems attempt to measure are the same as those which the human eye/brain system senses: position, geometric configuration, and light intensity distribution. Most commercial machine vision systems concentrate primarily on determining features relating to image shape, such as dimensions or edge location. Only in a limited number of actual production situations are commercial systems used to infer three-dimensional characteristics of objects or to analyze variations in light intensity over an image.

MACHINE VISION SENSING PROCESS

The ideal machine vision system would combine the accuracy, flexibility and speed of human vision with the consistency and reliability of an automated manufacturing system. However, the human system is extremely complex, and designing an artificial system is a difficult task. The human system interprets images by combining logical perceptual models with highly intuitive models based upon extensive symbolism. The human system also provides a continually updated flow of detailed information, much more than is normally required to interpret an image. To design a machine version of this sophisticated system, a greatly simplified model is used.

As discussed earlier, the ultimate goal of the image recognition process is to reduce ambiguities, or the number of ways in which an image can be interpreted, to a minimum. The human eye/brain system does this through a process which, although complex, does appear to have a systematic basis to it. An object will be recognized by generating the least amount of information required to establish identity within acceptable confidence limits. If simply determining the location of an object is sufficient to establish its identity, then no additional information is necessary. If the object's identity remains uncertain, however, then more complex information will be required, such as the identification of its two-dimensional shape. If necessary, further information can be gathered by analyzing subtle variations in light intensity on the surface of the object.

The extent of ambiguity in the image depends on such factors as the shape of the object, illumination, and the orientation of the surface of the object. Fortunately, many manufacturing applications require that only the most elementary information about workpieces be analyzed by a vision system. Inspection of subassemblies, for example, may only require that a vision system examine the silhouettes of two connected parts to determine if they are in the correct relative positions. In this case, the sensing process would not need to include an analysis of surface characteristics.

Regardless of the level of detail required in analyzing an image, the machine vision process consists of four basic steps, as shown in Exhibit 6. First, an image of a scene must be formed. Second, the image is processed to prepare it in a form suitable for computer analysis. Third, the characteristics of the image are defined and analyzed. Finally, the image is interpreted, conclusions are drawn, and a decision is made about some action to be taken, such as an accept/reject decision, a decision to sort or categorize an object, or a decision to make some movement.

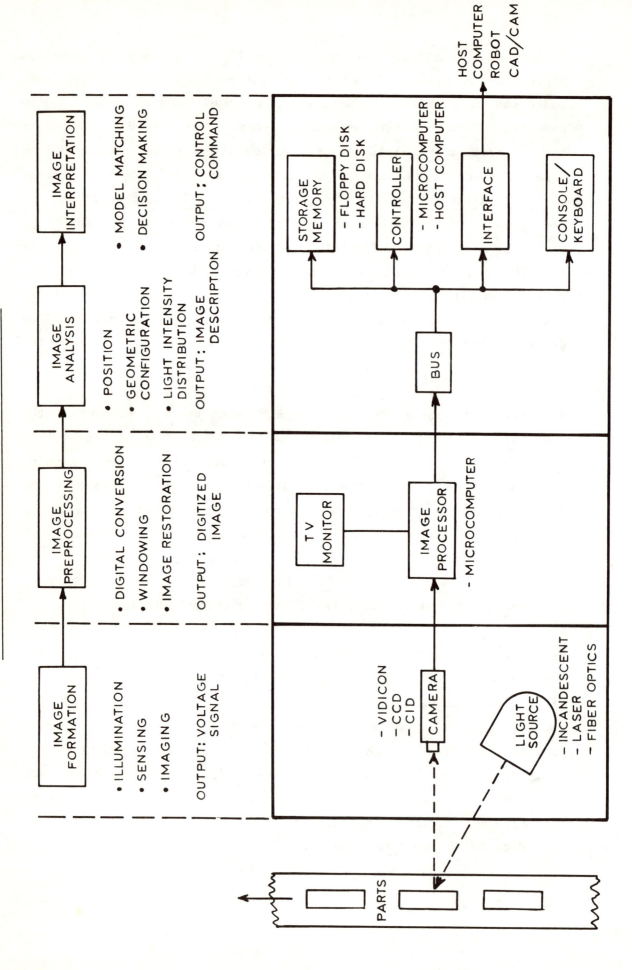

EXHIBIT 6

TYPICAL MACHINE VISION PROCESS

Image Formation

There are two primary differences between the way in which an image is formed by the human eye/brain system and by a machine vision system. First, the eye forms an analog image, while a computer requires discrete bits of data for analysis, and so a digital image is the appropriate machine vision counterpart. Second, the eye/brain system uses parallel processing to form an image, while a machine vision system sequentially forms the image, one bit at a time. This gives humans the ability to see an entire scene at once and form an immediate impression.

Illumination

The image formation process begins with the generation of light from the subject being observed. As discussed earlier, the quality of an image can be greatly affected by certain fundamental characteristics of the scene, such as the orientation of the subject or the nature of the source of illumination.

The correct placement of lighting can allow for adequate contrast at image boundaries being studied, as shown in Exhibit 7. When a simple silhouette image is all that is required, back lighting may be used for maximum contrast. If certain key surface features must be studied, such as a label on a container, front lighting would be used. If an object is to be inspected to insure that certain three-dimensional features are present, some form of side lighting might be required. For example, a flat plate with a vertical bar welded to its surface could be viewed with side lighting, first to examine its boundaries, and then to study the shape of the dark shadow cast by the vertical bar. This would determine whether or not the right shape of bar has been attached as well as its location.

EXHIBIT 7

ILLUMINATION TECHNIQUES

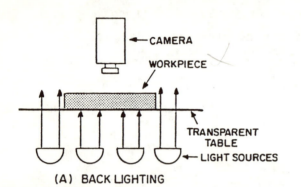

(A) BACK LIGHTING

(D) FRONT LIGHTING-DIRECTED BRIGHT FIELD

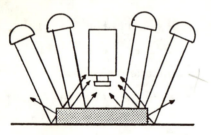

(B) FRONT LIGHTING-DIFFUSE

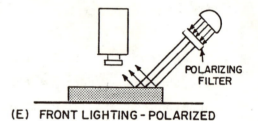

(E) FRONT LIGHTING-POLARIZED

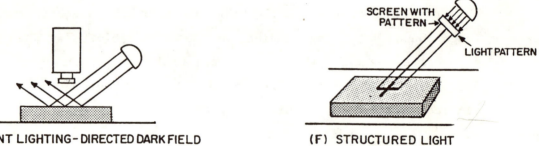

(C) FRONT LIGHTING-DIRECTED DARK FIELD

(F) STRUCTURED LIGHT

Typical light sources used in manufacturing operations include incandescent lights, fluorescent tubes, fiber optics, arc lamps, and strobe lights. In addition, laser beams are used for special imaging applications, such as the use of structured light or the use of triangulation as a means of measuring distance to an object. Occasionally, polarized or ultraviolet light is used to reduce glare or increase contrast.

Proper orientation of the part is also important. An idealized machine vision system would be able to interpret surface shadings and shadows for any orientation of a part, but today's real world systems require a certain amount of regularity in the way parts are presented.

Image Sensing

Once the scene has been properly arranged, an electronic imager acts as the sensing device for the system. The goal of the imager, like the human eye, is to create the basic image or two-dimensional representation of the scene, which is to be used for further processing and interpretation.

A number of different types of electronic imaging devices have been used in commercial versions of vision systems. An imaging device is a sensor which collects light from a scene (typically through a lens) and then converts the light into electrical energy through the use of some type of photosensitive target. Commercial machine vision systems employ imagers which generate images in the form of two-dimensional arrays, such as those formed by conventional TV cameras, or one-dimensional, linear arrays, which are used to create the image by scanning the scene one line at a time. Typical machine vision imagers are shown in Exhibit 8.

The most commonly used camera in early vision system models was the

EXHIBIT 8

TYPICAL IMAGE SENSORS

A) VIDICON CAMERA (COURTESY OF COHU, INC.)

B) CCD CAMERA (COURTESY OF FAIRCHILD)

C) REMOTE CID CAMERA (COURTESY OF GENERAL ELECTRIC)

D) MINIATURE CCD CAMERA (COURTESY OF SONY)

vidicon camera, which is extensively used in consumer video recorders. The vidicon camera has the advantage of providing a great deal of information about a scene at very fast speeds and at a relatively low cost (a typical camera costs several hundred dollars). An image is formed by focusing the incoming light through a series of lens onto the photoconductive faceplate of the vidicon tube. An electron beam within the tube scans this photoconductive surface and produces an analog output voltage proportional to the variations in light intensity for each scan line of the original scene. Normally, the output signal conforms to commercial TV standards, thus the total image is represented by 525 scan lines (interlaced into two fields of 262.5 lines), which is repeated 30 times per second.

The use of vidicon cameras for industrial machine vision applications does have several drawbacks, however. They tend to distort the image due to their construction and operation and are subject to image "burn-in" on the photoconductive surface. They also have limited useful lives and are susceptible to damage from vibration and shock.

Increasingly popular for state-of-the-art machine vision systems is the use of solid state cameras, which employ charge-coupled device (CCD) or charge-injected device (CID) image sensors. These sensors are fabricated on silicon chips using integrated circuit technology. They contain matrix or linear arrays of small, accurately spaced photosensitive elements. When light passing through the camera lens strikes the array, each detector converts the portion of light falling upon it into an analog electrical signal. The entire image is thus broken into an array of individual picture elements, also known as "pixels". The magnitude of the analog voltage registered for each pixel is directly proportional to the intensity of light in that portion of the image. This voltage represents an "average" of the light intensity variation over the area of the pixel. CCD and CID arrays differ primarily in how the voltages are extracted from the sensors.

Typical matrix array solid state cameras have 256x256 detector elements per array, although a number of other configurations, such as 128x128, 240x320 and 512x512 are also popular. The output from solid state matrix array cameras may or may not be compatible with commercial TV standards. Linear arrays may have from 256 to 1024 or more elements. The use of a linear array necessitates some type of mechanical scanning device, such as rotating mirrors, or workpiece motion, such as a part traveling on a conveyor, in order to generate a two-dimensional representation of an image. The type of solid state sensor and its configuration selected for a specific application will depend upon a number of factors, including the resolution required, lenses employed, lighting, cost and similar constraints.

In general, solid state cameras offer several important advantages over vidicon cameras. In addition to being smaller than vidicon cameras, solid state array cameras also are more rugged. The photosensitive surfaces in solid state cameras do not wear out with use as they do in vidicon cameras. Because of the accurate placement of the photo detectors, solid state cameras also exhibit less image distortion. On the other hand, solid state cameras are usually more expensive than vidicon cameras, although the cost of solid state cameras is expected to decline in the future.

A comparison of the advantages and disadvantages of the major camera types is contained in Exhibit 9. As the cost of solid state cameras decreases, they are expected to be widely used in industrial machine vision applications.

Machine vision cameras are manufactured by a variety of companies, including RCA, EG&G Reticon, and Fairchild. Except for GE, most vision system suppliers do not manufacture their own cameras, preferring instead to purchase them from other vendors. A listing of

EXHIBIT 9

COMPARISON OF TYPICAL IMAGE SENSORS

RANK (1 = BEST, 3 = WORST)

FEATURE	VIDICON	CCD	CID
RESOLUTION	1	2	2
SENSITIVITY	1	2	3
SPEED	3	2	1
BLOOM	3	2	1
SIZE	2	1	1
RELIABILITY	2	1	1
CURRENT COST	1	3	2
FUTURE COST	3	2	1

a number of camera suppliers is contained in Appendix A.

Although most machine vision systems use image sensors of the types described above, a few systems use special purpose sensors for limited applications. This would include, for example, specialty sensors for weld seam tracking and even ultrasonic sensors. These and other types of special sensors are touched upon in sections of the report.

Image Preprocessing

The initial sensing operation performed by the camera results in a series of voltage levels which represent light intensities over the area of the image. This preliminary image must then be processed so that it is presented to the microcomputer in a form suitable for analysis. A camera typically forms an image 30 to 60 times per second, or once every 33 to 17 milliseconds. At each time interval, the image is captured or "frozen" for processing by an image processor. The image processor, which is typically a microcomputer, transforms the analog voltage values for the image into corresponding digital values by means of an analog to digital converter. The result is an array of digital numbers which represent a light intensity distribution over the image area. This digital pixel array is then stored in memory until it is analyzed and interpreted.

Depending upon the number of possible digital values which can be assigned to each pixel, there are two general ways in which vision systems can be classified:

- Binary system - In this system, the voltage level for each pixel is assigned a digital value of 0 or 1, depending on whether the magnitude of the signal is less than or greater than some predetermined threshold level. The light intensity for each pixel is thus considered to be either white or black, depending on how light or dark the image is.

- Gray scale system - Like the binary system, the gray scale vision system assigns digital values to pixels, depending on whether or not certain voltage levels are exceeded. The difference is that a binary system allows two possible values to be assigned, while a gray scale system typically allows up to 256 different values. In addition to white or black, many different shades of gray can be distinguished. This greatly increased refinement capability enables gray scale systems to compare objects on the basis of such surface characteristics as texture, color, or surface orientation, all of which produce subtle variations in light intensity distributions. Gray scale systems are less sensitive to the placement of illumination than binary systems, in which threshold values can be affected by lighting.

As an example of gray scale image formation, the human eye has been digitized in Exhibit 10. The effect is similar to the dot pattern produced in a halftone photograph used in newspapers. Each square (or pixel) has a constant shade of gray over its entire area. When seen from a distance, the features of the human eye are clearly recognizable.

The effects of various levels of gray scale digitization are illustrated in Exhibit 11. The top photo depicts a binary (2 level) representation of an image. Although you can identify the scene, much of the detailed information is lost. In the middle photo, the same image is digitized into eight gray levels. At this level of detail you can begin to read the part number on the integrated circuit and

EXHIBIT 10

EXAMPLE OF GRAY SCALE IMAGE:
A DIGITIZED HUMAN EYE

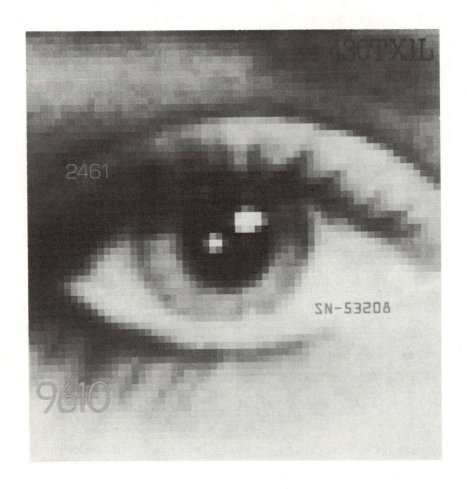

(PHOTO COURTESY COGNEX CORPORATION)

EXHIBIT 11

THE EFFECT OF VARIOUS LEVELS
OF GRAY SCALE DIGITIZATION

A) BINARY (2 LEVEL) IMAGE

B) EIGHT-LEVEL GRAY SCALE IMAGE

C) SIXTY-FOUR LEVEL GRAY SCALE IMAGE

(PHOTOS COURTESY OF COGNEX)

identify the individual circuit pads in the upper right hand portion of the photo. At 64 levels, as shown in the bottom photo, the image is fairly well defined.

Most commercial vision systems in use today are binary. For simple inspection tasks, silhouette images are adequate (for example, to determine if a part is missing or broken). However, gray scale systems are now beginning to be employed in some applications requiring a higher degree of image refinement. Example binary and gray scale systems are shown in Exhibits 12 and 13, respectively.

Unfortunately, you cannot always rely on a vendor's literature to determine whether a particular machine vision system is binary or gray scale. Several vendors describe their systems as gray scale, when in fact the image processing is done only on a binary representation of the image. The reason they call their systems gray scale (beyond wanting to sell more systems) is because the image representation from the camera may be digitized into more than two levels for some reason, such as to establish a binary threshold level, even though the image is ultimately converted into a binary representation. Such "pseudo" gray scale systems do not have the same capabilities as true gray scale systems.

One of the most fundamental challenges to the widespread usage of true gray scale systems is the greatly increased computer processing requirements relative to those of binary systems. A 256x256 pixel image array with up to 256 different values per pixel will require over 65,000 8-bit storage locations for analysis. At a speed of 30 images per second, the data processing requirement becomes very large, which means that the time required to process large amounts of data can be significant. Ideally, a vision system should be capable of real time processing and interpretation of an image, particularly when the system is used for on-line inspection or guidance and control of equipment such as robots.

BINARY VISION SYSTEM:
THE IMAGER 3000 FROM IMAGE
DATA SYSTEMS

EXHIBIT 12

(COURTESY OF IMAGE DATA SYSTEMS, INC.)

GRAY SCALE VISION SYSTEM:
THE IVS 100 FROM ANALOG DEVICES

EXHIBIT 13

(COURTESY OF ANALOG DEVICES)

One approach to reducing the amount of data to be processed, and therefore the time, is through a process known as windowing. This process creates an electronic mask around a small area of an image to be studied. Only the pixels that are not blocked out will be analyzed by the computer. This technique is especially useful for such simple inspection applications as the determination of whether or not a certain part has been attached to another part. Rather than process the entire image, a window can be created over the area where the attached part is expected to be located. By simply counting the number of pixels of a certain intensity within the window, a quick determination can be made of whether or not the part is present. A window can be virtually any size, from one pixel up to a major portion of the image. The result of windowing can be a substantial reduction in processing time.

Another way in which the image can be prepared in a more suitable form during the preprocessing step is through the techniques of image restoration. Very often an image suffers various forms of degradation, such as blurring of lines or boundaries, poor contrast between image regions, or the presence of background noise. There are several possible causes of image degradation, including: motion of the camera or object during image formation; poor illumination or improper placement of illumination; variations in sensor response; or the very common problem of defects or poor contrast on the surface of the subject, such as deformed letters on labels or overlapping parts with similar light intensities. There are a number of techniques for improving the quality of an image, such as:

- Constant brightness addition - This approach simply adds a constant amount of brightness to each pixel, which may improve the contrast in the image.

- Contrast stretching - This increases the relative contrast between high and low intensity elements by making light pixels lighter and dark pixels darker.

- <u>Fourier-domain processing</u> - This powerful technique is based on the principle that changes in brightness in an image can be represented as a series of sine and cosine waves. These waves can be described by specifying amplitudes and frequencies in a series of equations. By breaking the image down into its sinusoidal components, each component image wave can be acted upon separately. Changing the magnitude of certain component waves will result in a sharper image, much the way musical recordings are improved by altering either the treble or bass component separately. The result can be a less blurred image, better defined edges or lines, greater contrast between regions, or a reduction in background noise. In other words, the image becomes crisper.

Some machine vision systems perform additional operations as part of the preprocessing function in order to facilitate image analysis or reduce memory storage requirements. These operations differ according to the specific system and are largely dependent on the analysis technique employed in later stages of the process.

One such operation is known as edge detection. An "edge" is a boundary within an image where there is a dramatic change in light intensity between adjacent pixels. These boundaries usually correspond to real edges on the workpiece being examined by the vision system, and thus are very important for such applications as inspection of part dimensions. Edges are usually determined by using one of a number of different "gradient" operators which mathematically calculate the presence of an edge point by weighting the intensity value of pixels surrounding the point. The resulting edges represent a skeleton of the outline of the parts contained in the original image. Some vision systems include" thinning," "gap filling," and "curve smoothing" to insure that the detected edges are only one pixel wide, they are continuous in nature and they are appropriately shaped. Rather than storing the entire image in memory, the vision system stores only the edges or some symbolic representation of the edges, thereby dramatically reducing the amount of memory required.

"Run length encoding" is another preprocessing operation used in some vision systems. This operation is similar to edge detection in binary images. In run length encoding, each line of the image is scanned and transition points from black to white or white to balck are noted, along with the number of pixels between transitions. This run length data is then stored in memory instead of the original image and serves as the starting point for the image analysis phase. One of the earliest and most widely used vision techniques, originally developed by Stanford Research Institute and known as the SRI algorithms, uses run length encoded image data.

The techniques mentioned above are but a few of those employed in commercial machine vision systems. The specific preprocessing operations used depend on the application involved and the subsequent image analysis approach used by the system. These preprocessing operations have a significant effect on the design, performance and cost of vision systems.

Image Analysis

The third general step in the vision sensing process is to analyze the digital image that has been formed so that conclusions can be drawn and decisions can be made. This is normally performed in the system's central processing unit (CPU), such as a microcomputer. The image is analyzed by describing and measuring the properties of several image features. These features may belong to the image as a whole or to regions of the image. In general, machine vision systems begin the process of image interpretation by analyzing the simplest features and then adding more complicated features until the image is clearly identified. A large number of different techniques are either used or being developed for use in commercial vision systems to analyze the image features describing the object's position, its geometric configuration, and the distribution of light intensity over the visible surface of the object.

Position

There are many manufacturing applications in which it is not important to determine the position of a part, such as when inspecting a conveyor line of uniform parts that are rigidly positioned. However, in more complex operations, such as when a workpiece must be positioned relative to a mating part, it may be essential to monitor the location and orientation of the part in space. A two-dimensional example is a group of flat parts that are randomly placed along a conveyor line. In this case, a camera viewing the line from above would need to determine the position of each part along with its orientation.

Determining the position of a part with a known orientation and distance from the camera is one of the simpler tasks a machine vision system can perform. As an example, consider the case of locating a round washer laying on a table so that it can be grasped by a robot. In this case, a stationary camera could be used to obtain an image of the washer. The washer's position could then be determined by the vision system through an analysis of the pattern of the black and white pixels in the image. This position information would then be transmitted to the robot's controller, which would calculate an appropriate trajectory for the robot's arm. In many instances, however, neither the distance between the part and the camera nor the part's orientation are known, and the machine vision system's task is much more difficult.

The distance (or range) of an object from a vision system camera can be determined in several ways, none of which are widely used yet in manufacturing operations(see Exhibit 14):

- Stadimetry - Also known as direct imaging, this is a technique for measuring distance based upon the apparent size of an object in the camera's field of view (see Exhibit 14(a). The farther away the object, the smaller will be its apparent image. This approach requires an accurate focusing of the image. It also requires an accurate determination of two known locations on the image surface, such as the centers of two holes. This will minimize errors due to imprecise edge location.

- Triangulation - This accurate technique is based on the measurement of the base line of a right triangle formed by the light path to the object, the reflected light path to the camera, and a line from the camera to the light source, as seen in Exhibit 14(b). A typical light source for this technique is a light emitting diode (LED) or laser to form a well-defined spot of light. The angle between the two light paths is preset, and the distance L is measured, so distance D is readily calculated. If the object moves from A to B, distances D and L both increase proportionately. Typical accuracies of one micrometer can be achieved with this technique. However, it is difficult to prevent occlusions from interferring with the light path, such as those caused by the edges at the rim of a hole when measuring hole depth. Deep hole depths are therefore difficult to measure using this method.

EXHIBIT 14

TECHNIQUES FOR MEASURING DISTANCE
WITH MACHINE VISION

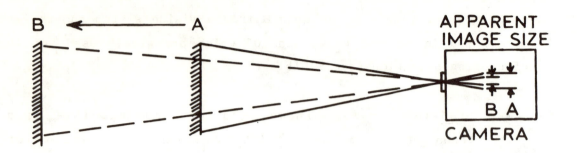

(a)   STADIMETRY (DIRECT IMAGING)

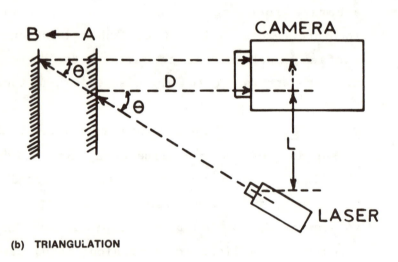

(b)   TRIANGULATION

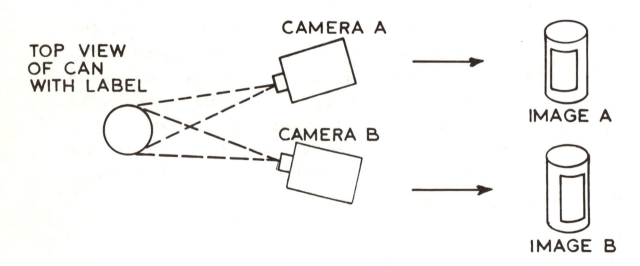

(c)   STEREO (BINOCULAR VISION)

- <u>Stereo</u> - Also known as binocular vision, this method uses the principle of parallax to measure distance. Parallax is the change in the relative perspective of a scene as the observer (or camera) moves. The human eyes provides the best example of stereo vision. The right eye views an object as if the object were rotated slightly from the position observed by the left eye (see Exhibit 14(c)). Also, an object in front of another object seems to move relative to the other object when seen from one eye and then from the other. The closer the objects, the greater is the parallax. A practical stereo machine vision system is not yet available, in large part because of the difficulty of matching the two different images which are formed by two different views of the same object.

Orientation of objects in manufacturing environments is important to determine in such operations as material handling or assembly, where a robot may need to correctly position itself relative to a part in order to grasp it and transfer it to another location. Several methods can be used for determining orientation:

- <u>Equivalent ellipse</u> - For an image of an object in a two-dimensional plane, an ellipse can be calculated which has the same area as the image. The major axis of the ellipse will define the object's orientation. Another similar measure is the axis of least moment of inertia.

- <u>Connecting three points</u> - If the relative positions of three noncolinear points in a surface are known, the orientation of the surface in space can be determined by measuring the apparent relative position of the points in the image.

51

- <u>Light intensity distribution</u> - As discussed in Chapter 1, a surface will appear darker if it is oriented at an angle other than normal to the light source. Determining orientation based upon relative light intensity requires a knowledge of the source of illumination as well as the surface characteristics of the object.

- <u>Structured light</u> - As the name implies, structured light involves the use of a light pattern rather than a diffused light source. The workpiece is illuminated by the structured light and the way in which the pattern is distorted by the part can be used to determine both the three-dimensional shape and orientation of the part.

The position of an object is also defined by its relative motion. Certain operations, such as tracking or part insertion, may require that a vision system be capable of following the motion of an object. This is a difficult task which requires that a series of image frames be compared for relative changes in position during specified time intervals. Motion in one dimension, as in the case of a moving conveyor of parts, is the least complicated motion to detect. In two-dimensions, motion may consist of both a rotational and a translational component. In three dimensions, a total of six motion components may need to be defined (three rotational axes and three translational axes). A high speed of motion causes additional difficulties if the motion is more complex than a simple linear displacement. Processing speed limitations for complex images may restrict the ability of a vision system to track high speed motions. One way to freeze images during motion is through the use of a strobe light, which can produce several hundred images per second.

Geometric Configuration

One of the more useful approaches to image interpretation in real world manufacturing operations is the analysis of fundamental geometric properties of two-dimensional images. The reason that machine vision systems, are being increasingly employed in manufacturing operations is that typical parts tend to have distinct shapes that can be recognized on the basis of very elementary features. Very often these distinguishing features are simple enough to allow identification independent of the orientation of the part. For example, if surface area (number of pixels) is the only feature required to differentiate parts, then orientation of the part is not important. For more complex three-dimensional objects, additional geometric properties may need to be determined, including descriptions of various image segments. The process of determining these elementary properties of the image is often referred to as feature extraction. The first step is to determine boundary locations and segment the image into distinct regions. Next, certain geometric properties of these regions are determined. Finally, these image regions are organized in a structure describing their relationships:

- <u>Image segmentation</u> - This step, is extremely difficult for a machine vision system. Apparent discontinuities in an image may not correspond to actual physical boundaries in an object. Shadows caused by the placement of lighting or by occlusions can be difficult for machine vision systems to interpret. The simplest case in a manufacturing environment is that of a part with a uniform surface and no occlusions. In this case, there is only one image region, with one well-defined boundary. This common situation is ideal for a binary system, which can easily detect edges by scanning the image for abrupt light intensity changes.

  For more complex images, a gray scale system may be more suitable, such as when two adjacent regions have nearly the same light intensity (for example, a raised set of numbers on the surface of a tire). A boundary can be defined as a sudden change in intensity (gradient) which exceeds a certain threshold level. In a gray scale system, regions are formed by clustering adjacent pixels which have nearly the same level of intensity. This technique is known as the "nearest neighbor" approach. If a pixel falls above or below a specified range, a new region is assumed to start. This process continues until the image has been reduced to a series of well-defined lines and regions. In addition, these boundaries may be further smoothed, noise may be eliminated, or gaps in boundaries caused by occlusions may be filled in, using a number of techniques for "cleaning up" the data.

- Imaging shape - Either the silhouette outline of the image or the shapes of certain segments may provide the information necessary to interpret the image. The simplest feature to measure, and one which applies to a large number of objects, is the area of the image. This applies when an object can be differentiated from other objects solely on the basis of image size. This approach can be used for many inspection applications, such as monitoring items for missing or broken parts. A series of assemblies can be inspected to insure that a certain part is always present by windowing the image to measure only the portion where the part should be present.

More complex objects may require that additional features be analyzed, such as the perimeter of the image (or a region), centroid, dimensions, major axis, curvature of certain lines, moment of inertia, number of holes, and so forth. The specific set of features to be measured depends upon the degree of ambiguity in the image. Segmenting an image into distinct regions of constant light intensity allows a large number of combinations of features to be examined.

In every case, image features are measured through simple arithmetic calculations based upon the number of pixels and their location in the image.

- Image organization - The various image components (regions and boundaries), along with descriptions of corresponding features, can be structured by the vision system in a hierarchical or tree-like fashion, in which image components are listed along with calculated values for each and relationships among them. As discussed in Chapter 1, it is often possible to infer three-dimensional object structure based upon the hierarchical relationships of the components of the image.

Light Intensity Distribution

One of the most sophisticated and potentially useful approaches to machine vision is the interpretation of an image based upon the difference in intensity of light in different regions. Many of the features described above are used in current vision systems to make two-dimensional interpretations of images. However, analysis of subtle changes in shadings over the image can add a great deal of information about the three-dimensional nature of the object. The problem is that most machine vision techniques are not capable of dealing with the complex patterns formed by varying conditions of illumination, surface texture and color, and surface orientation.

Another more fundamental difficulty is that imager intensities can change drastically with relatively modest variations in illumination or surface conditions. Systems which attempt to match gray level values of each pixel to a stored model can easily suffer deterioration in performance in real world manufacturing environments. The use of geometric features such as edges or boundaries is therefore likely to remain the preferred approach for some time. Even better approaches are likely to result from research being performed on various techniques for determining surface shapes from relative intensity levels. One approach being studied at the Massachusetts Institute of Technology, for example, assumes that the light intensity at a given point on the surface of an object can be precisely determined by an equation describing the nature and location of the light source, the orientation of the surface at the point, and the reflectivity of the surface.

Image Interpretation

When the system has completed the process of analyzing image features, some conclusion must be made about the findings, such as the verification that a part is or is not present, the identification of an object based upon recognition of its image, or the establishment that certain parameters of the object fall within acceptable limits. Based upon these conclusions, certain decisions can then be made about the object or the production process. These conclusions are formed by comparing the results of the analysis with a prestored set of standard criteria. These standard criteria describe the expected characteristics of the image, and are developed either through a programmed model of the image or by building an average profile of previously examined objects.

In the simplest case of a binary system, the process of comparing an image with standard criteria may simply require that all white and black pixels within a certain area be counted. Once the image is segmented (windowed), all groups of black pixels within each segment that are connected (called blobs) are identified and counted. The same process is followed for groups of white pixels (called holes).

The number of blobs, holes, and pixels are counted and compared with expected numbers to determine how closely the real image matches the standard image. If the numbers are within a certain percentage of each other, it can be assumed that there is a match. This is an example of a statistical approach to image interpretation.

A simple example of this approach is the identification of a part on the basis of a known outline, such as the center hole of a washer. As seen in Exhibit 15, a simple 3x3 pixel window can be used to locate the hole of the washer and distinguish the washer from other distinctly different washers. The dark pixels in Exhibit 15(a) represent the rough shape of the washer. When the window is centered on the shape, all nine pixels are assigned a value of "0" (white). In Exhibit 15(b), a defective washer appears, with the hole skewed to the right. The window now only counts six white pixels, and so it can be assumed that the hole is incorrectly formed. In Exhibit 15(c), a second washer category is introduced, one with a smaller hole. In this case, only five white pixels are counted, which is enough information to identify the washer as a different type. In Exhibit 15(d), a third washer is inspected, one that is larger than the first. The window counts nine white pixels, as in Exhibit 15(a). in this case, some ambiguity remains, and so additional information would be required, such as the use of a 5x5 window. Another approach is to count all the black pixels rather than the white ones.

In this simplified example, a positive identification of the washer (or the assumption of a defect) is possible through a minimum amount of data processing. By counting the white pixels, a very rough approximation of the area of the hole is determined. If this area is too small, then either the hole is not formed correctly, or the washer belongs to a different category of washers. This is an example of image interpretation on the basis of a statistical analysis of one image feature (area).

EXHIBIT 15

EXAMPLES OF BINARY INTERPRETATION OF WASHERS USING WINDOWING

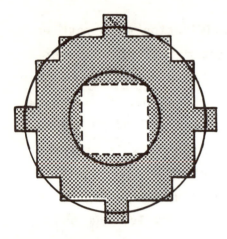

(a) STANDARD WASHER: 9 WHITE PIXELS IN WINDOW

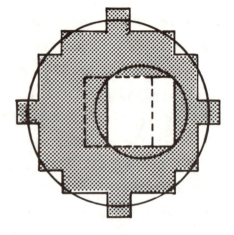

(b) WASHER WITH OFF-CENTER HOLE: 6 WHITE PIXELS IN WINDOW

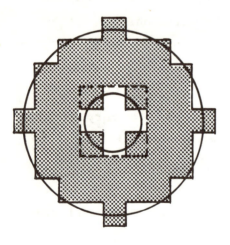

(c) WASHER WITH SMALL HOLE: 5 WHITE PIXELS IN WINDOW

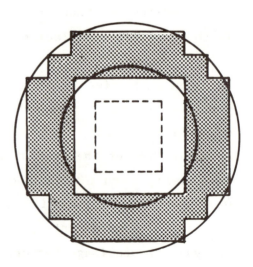

(d) LARGE WASHER: 9 WHITE PIXELS IN WINDOW; NEED LARGER WINDOW.

The reason that such simple methods are finding useful applications in manufacturing environments is because of the controlled, structured nature of most manufacturing environments. The amount of analysis required for part recognition depends on both the complexity of the image and the goal of the analysis. In a manufacturing situation, the complexity of the image is often greatly reduced by controlling such factors as illumination, part location, and part orientation. The goal of the analysis is simplified when parts have easily identifiable features, such as in the washer example.

In order for machine vision systems to achieve widespread usage, however, much more sophisticated image analysis techniques are required. A major reason for using a vision system is to eliminate the need for elaborate jigs and fixtures. A sophisticated vision system can offer a great deal of flexibility by reducing the amount of structure required in presenting parts for inspection. But as structure is reduced, the relative complexity of the image increases (i.e., the degree of ambiguity increases). This includes such additional complexities as overlapping parts, randomly aligned parts, and parts that are only distinguishable on the basis of differences in surface features.

In such situations, there are two general ways in which image interpretation capabilities are being improved in today's vision systems: gray scale image interpretation, and the use of various algorithms for complex analysis of image data. The use of gray scale image analysis greatly increases the quality of data available for interpreting an image. The use of advanced data analysis algorithms improves the way in which the data is interpreted. Both of these approaches allow the interpretation of much more complex images than the simple washer inspection example described above.

However, even gray scale image analysis and sophisticated data analysis algorithms do not provide absolute interpretation of images.

Machine vision deals in probabilities, and the goal is to achieve a probability of correct interpretation as close to 100% as possible. In complex situations, the human system is vastly superior to machine systems. However, in many simple manufacturing operations, where inspection is performed over long periods of time, the overall percentage of correct conclusions can be higher for machines than for humans, who are subject to fatigue.

The two most commonly used methods of interpreting images are the following:

- Feature weighting - In cases in which several image features must be measured in order to interpret an image, a simple factor weighting method may be used to consider the relative contribution of each feature to the analysis. For example, in order to identify a valve stem from among a group of stems of several sizes, the image area may not be sufficient by itself to ensure a positive identification. The measurement of height may add some additional information, as may the determination of the centroid of the image. Each feature would be compared with a standard for a goodness-of-fit measurement. Features that are known to be the most likely indicators of a match would be weighted more than others. A weighted total goodness-of-fit score could then be determined to indicate the likelihood that the object has been correctly identified.

- Template matching - In this method, a mask is electronically generated to match a standard image of an object. When the system inspects other objects in an attempt to recognize them, it aligns the image of each object with that of the standard object. In the case of a perfect match, all pixels would align perfectly. If the objects are not precisely the same, some pixels will fall outside of the standard image. The percentage of pixels in the two images which match is a measure of the goodness-of-fit. A threshold value can then be assigned to test for "pass" (positive match) or "reject" (no match). A probability factor, which presents the degree of confidence that a correct interpretation has been made, is normally calculated along with the go/no-go conclusion.

Variations of these two approaches are used in most commercially available vision systems today. Although conceptually simple, they can give powerful results in a variety of manufacturing applications requiring the identification of two dimensional parts with well-defined silhouettes.

With either method, a training session is usually conducted for the machine before actual use. During this session, several sample known parts are presented to the machine for analysis. The part features are stored and updated as each part is presented until the machine is "familiar" with the part. Then the actual production parts are studied by comparing with this stored model of a standard part.

Although model building, or programming, is generally accomplished by presenting a known sample object to the machine for analysis, it is also possible to create a mathematical model describing the expected image. This is generally applicable for objects which have well-defined shapes, such as rectangles or circles, especially if the descriptive data already exists in an off-line CAD/CAM data base. For example, the geometry of a rectangular machined part with several circular holes of known diameters and locations can be readily programmed. More complex shapes may be difficult to describe mathematically, and so it may be easier to teach the machine by allowing it to analyze a sample part. Most commercial systems include standard image processing software for calculating basic image features and comparing with models. However, custom programming for model generation can be designed either by the purchaser or by the vision system supplier. Off-line programming is likely to become increasingly popular as CAD/CAM interface methods improve.

Although the techniques described above apply to many if not most of the machine vision systems that are commercially available today, there are still other approaches being used by some suppliers, particularly for special purpose systems for such applications as printed circuit board (PCB) inspection, weld seam tracking, robot guidance and control, and inspection of microelectronic devices and tooling. These special purpose systems often incorporate unique image analysis and interpretation techniques which exploit constraints inherent in the applications.

For example, some PCB inspection systems employ image analysis algorithms based on "design rules" rather than feature weighting or template matching. In the design rule approach, the inspection process is based on known characteristics of a good product. For PCB's this would include minimum conductor width and spacing between conductors. Also, each conductor should end with a solder pad if the board is correct. If these rules are not complied with, then the product is rejected.

Interfacing

A machine vision system will rarely be used without some form of interaction with other factory equipment, such as CAD/CAM devices, robots, or host computers. This interaction is the final element of the machine vision process, in which conclusions about the image are translated into actions. In some cases, the final action may take the form of cumulative storage of information in a host computer, such as counting the numbers of parts in various categories for inventory control. In other situations, a final action may be a specific motion, such as the transfer of parts into different conveyors, depending on their characteristics. The use of vision systems for control purposes is increasingly being performed through the combination of vision systems and robots. In this case, the vision system acts to greatly expand the flexibility of the robot.

For most applications, interfacing a machine vision system with other equipment is a straightforward task. Most systems come equipped with a number of input and output ports, including a standard RS232C interface. When it comes to connecting a vision system to a robot, however, the task is much more complicated due to timing constraints, data formats and the inability of most robot controllers to handle vision system inputs. To overcome this problem, several robot and vision system manufacturers have developed integrated system capabilities.

PERFORMANCE CHARACTERISTICS

The components of a vision system and the process by which these components work together to form, analyze, and interpret an image describe the basic principles of machine vision. In addition to understanding how machine vision works, it is also useful to understand the basic criteria by which machine vision systems can be evaluated and compared. These represent the basic considerations that potential users should review when deciding which vision system to select for a particular application.

In general, the ideal system is one which allows fast, accurate interpretation of a wide variety of complex images with a minimum of

jigs and fixturing. Some of the more important performance
characteristics that should be considered include the following:

- Resolution - The ability of a vision system to resolve, or
  create a recognizable image from a particular feature of an
  object or scene, is directly determined by the number of
  pixels in the image array and the image sensor's field of
  view. For a standard array of 256x256 pixels, the system
  can resolve portions of an object which just fit into the
  field of view down to a size of 1/256 of either the
  horizontal or vertical dimension of the object. If the
  object is one inch long, the system will be able to
  perceive pieces of the object as small as .0039" (0.39%).
  For an array of 512x512 pixels, resolution would improve to
  .0020" (0.2%). Resolution for a given array can be
  improved by using a camera lens with a higher
  magnification, but the field of view will then shrink.

- Processing speed - A machine vision system should be
  capable of forming an image, analyzing it, and interpreting
  it at a speed consistent with the speed at which parts are
  being presented. Two categories of speed can be
  considered. First, image processing speed measures the
  number of bits of information which can be processed by the
  image processor. More important during an on-line
  application, however, is the speed at which individual
  items can be examined by the system. This is a difficult
  number to determine, since processing time is affected by
  many factors, such as the complexity of the image, the
  type of illumination, the accuracy required in interpreting
  an image and whether or not windowing is employed. Typical
  vision systems can inspect and recognize simple parts at
  rates of 2-10 items per second, with some achieving speeds
  of 15 parts per second and higher. Solid state CCD cameras

can achieve higher speeds than vidicon cameras. The speed of a vision system will be inversely proportional to the amount of information, or number of pixels, being analyzed. For character recognition systems, which read alphanumeric characters on parts, speeds of 5-15 characters per second are typical.

- Discrimination - The ability of a vision system to discriminate variations in light intensity over an image (i.e., contrast) is determined by the number of intensity thresholds present in the system. A binary system, which allows two levels of intensity, provides the least discriminative ability. A gray scale system is able to perceive more subtle intensity variations, with 16 level gray scale systems offering the highest degree of discrimination of commonly used machine vision systems. The trade-off is that better discriminaton means increased processing time along with a higher computer memory capacity.

- Accuracy - A trade-off can be made between processing speeds and the ablity to correctly interpret images. A higher probability of correct interpretation can be achieved by processing more image features, which increases the processing time. Accuracy, also known as reliability or consistency, can be defined as the percentage of correct decisions made about a group of objects being examined by a vision system. This is a difficult number to estimate, since it is a function of the variability of the objects, scene conditions such as illumination, the amount of teaching performed on the system, the adequacy of the standard model used for teaching or programming, and many other factors. An acceptable accuracy rate (90%, 95%, etc.) depends on the accuracy required by the application, as in any quality control situation.

CHAPTER 3
VISION SYSTEM APPLICATIONS

Machine vision systems can be considered for use in most manufacturing applications in which human vision is now required. Human vision is required for applications where non-contact feedback is used to provide information about a production process or a part. For example, a human welder or machinist uses visual feedback to insure that the correct relationship is maintained between the tool and the workpiece. Human assemblers visually analyze the position of parts so that other parts can be correctly aligned for insertion or some other form of mating. Quality control inspectors visually check products or parts to insure that there are no defects, such as missing parts, damage, or incorrect location of various features.

The primary strength of human vision is in its ability to analyze qualitative aspects of an object or a scene. However, humans are not particularly adept at measuring quantitative data. For example, although human vision uses a sophisticated approach for depth perception which allows it to correctly determine relative distances of objects, it is not able to measure a specific distance to an object other than as a very rough estimate. Similarly, human vision can measure dimensions only approximately. Humans must rely on some standard frame of reference for judging an object. A standard stored in the brain's memory does not provide a very good frame of reference from which to make quantitative measurements. It is not absolute, and it will vary from individual to individual. Humans are also subject to fatigue, so that interpretation of a standard may change over time.

Machine vision systems are ideally suited for a number of

applications in which their ability to consistently interpret images over long periods of time makes them perform better than humans.

Machine vision systems are also beginning to be used in many new and unique applications that simply did not exist previously. This includes, for example, on-line inspections that were not economically feasible before, and the use of machine vision to increase manufacturing flexibility and reduce dependence on expensive hard tooling. The net result is both improved product quality and lower production costs.

The decision of whether or not machine vision makes sense in a particular application must consider the capabilities of machine vision versus the requirements of the application. Although many applications are suitable for automated vision sensing, there are several complex applications in which the sophisticated recognition capability of human vision is better, such as inspection of certain complex three-dimensional objects.

FEASIBILITY CRITERIA

To be feasible for use in a particular manufacturing application, a machine vision system must be able to correctly interpret an image with a satisfactory degree of reliability. Assuming this fundamental criterion can be satisfied, then the system must be compared with the use of human vision or other sensing techniques to determine if machine vision can perform a task with higher accuracy or lower cost than its counterparts.

The evaluation of a machine vision system's applicability to a manufacturing operation requires that three basic criteria be considered. First, the fundamental system capabilities must be evaluated. Capabilities are the specific functions which the system can perform. These include recognition of an object and measurement of various object features, such as position or shape.

The determination that a vision system is capable of performing certain functions provides information on what the system can do. But a second consideration is how well the system can perform these functions. As discussed in Chapter 2, there are several fundamental performance criteria which can be used to evaluate a vision system, including operating speed, accuracy, resolution, and discrimination. In addition, a measure of operating cost or payback should be evaluated when considering a specific application.

The third consideration is the requirements of the application. Each application requires that a vision system have certain capabilities and be able to achieve certain levels of performance. For example, an inspection operation in which objects with subtle differences in surface markings are to be differentiated may require a vision system with gray scale surface interpretation capabilities. Or a certain quality control application may require that a vision system be able to correctly read product labels with 99% accuracy. Only when application requirements are evaluated against vision system capabilities and performance levels can a true feasibility assessment be made.

In general, the requirements of an application are determined by the nature of the manufacturing environment within which the application is performed. This includes the following characteristics:

- Scene complexity – This includes the number of objects in the scene, characteristics of the illumination, degree of overlap of objects, and the nature of the light distribution over the surface of the objects resulting from object shapes. Highly complex scenes will require sophisticated vision system analysis capabilities and performance levels.

- Part differentiation - The greater the degree of similarity among different classes of parts, the greater will be the need for a strong vision system discrimination capability.

- Degree of structure - A fundamental reason for using automated vision systems is to reduce the need for an orderly, highly structured presentation of parts. However, as parts are presented in a less structured manner, increasing demands are placed on the capabilities of the vision system.

- Production volume - Generally, machine vision systems can be economically justified when used in manufacturing operations in which production volumes are high. However, they are also suitable for medium volume operations in certain situations. For example, if 100% inspection is required on critical parts, machine vision may be used to insure a high degree of accuracy. When used as vision feedback for robots, vision systems may also be used in the medium volume operations normally associated with robots. Vision systems may also be used in certain low volume operations. For example, they may be used to inspect large, complex castings which would require several hours for a human operator to inspect.

- Production rate - With today's vision systems able to analyze objects at a typical rate of about 2-10 items per second, the rate at which parts are presented becomes an important factor. Also, if the part is moving, the speed of motion can be a limiting factor on the vision system's performance. High speeds can cause image blurring, which must then be corrected by the system for clarification.

- Reliability requirement - Finally, depending on the nature of the part, each application will require that a minimum level of accuracy be achieved in interpreting an image. In some situations, a vision system may not be able to achieve a high reliability percentage because of the factors discussed above. In these cases, human vision or some other recognition process may be required.

MACHINE VISION VS. HUMAN VISION

In many situations, an automated vision system will be suitable for a specific application only if it will perform a task better than a human operator. In general, a machine vision system will be more suitable for an application than a human in one of three situations:

- When machine vision has capabilities that humans do not.

- When machine vision offers better performance than humans, such as higher inspection speeds or lower error rate.

- When a visual inspection or feedback task is unpleasant or hazardous for humans to perform.

One way of deciding whether a machine vision system is more suitable than a human for a particular application is to judge each on the basis of the criteria discussed above. As seen in Exhibit 16, there are certain tradeoffs in comparing the capabilities of machine and human vision systems. Today's machine vision systems have limited

71

EXHIBIT 16

MACHINE VISION VS. HUMAN VISION: EVALUATION OF CAPABILITIES

CAPABILITIES	MACHINE VISION	HUMAN VISION
DISTANCE	LIMITED CAPABILITIES	GOOD QUALITATIVE CAPABILITIES
ORIENTATION	GOOD FOR 2-D	GOOD QUALITATIVE CAPABILITIES
MOTION	LIMITED, SENSITIVE TO IMAGE BLURRING	GOOD QUALITATIVE CAPABILITIES
EDGES/REGIONS	HIGH CONTRAST IMAGE REQUIRED	HIGHLY DEVELOPED
IMAGE SHAPES	GOOD QUANTITATIVE MEASUREMENTS	QUALITATIVE ONLY
IMAGE ORGANIZATION	SPECIAL SOFTWARE NEEDED; LIMITED CAPABILITY	HIGHLY DEVELOPED
SURFACE SHADING	LIMITED CAPABILITY WITH GRAY SCALE	HIGHLY DEVELOPED
2-D INTERPRETATION	EXCELLENT FOR WELL DEFINED FEATURES	HIGHLY DEVELOPED
3-D INTERPRETATION	VERY LIMITED CAPABILITIES	HIGHLY DEVELOPED
OVERALL:	BEST FOR QUANTITATIVE MEASUREMENT OF STRUCTURED SCENE	BEST FOR QUALITATIVE INTERPRETATION OF COMPLEX, UNSTRUCTURED SCENE

capabilities to deal with complex images. Human vision, on the other hand, has a highly developed capability to interpret complex, ambiguous images. In many manufacturing applications, however, images are fairly simple, and the process of image interpretation requires accurate measurement of features rather than symbolic inferences. When images are well defined, machine vision has much better measurement capabilities than humans. For manufactured parts with well defined tolerances, machine vision systems can measure image features more consistently than humans, even when humans use accurate gages. Humans are capable of achieving better qualitative measurements, such as relative positions or orientations of three-dimensional objects.

As a result, humans can often achieve better performance than machine systems when inspecting one part, as seen in Exhibit 17. Humans have better resolution than machine vision systems, they can process images in real time, and they can interpret images where the contrast between regions is nearly zero. However, machine vision system performance improves considerably when either a large number of separate parts are being examined or a large number of elements of a very complex assembly are being measured as in an engine block. Humans are subject to fatigue and increasing error rates over long periods of time, while machine vision system performance remains constant. For large production volumes or a large number of items to be inspected on one part, machine vision operating costs tend to become lower than those for humans, and reliability tends to be higher. In addition, overall productivity is likely to be higher for machine vision systems.

At the present time, human vision tends to outperform machine vision in applications in which a complex, unstructured scene is being examined, a qualitative rather than quantitative interpretation of the scene is required, and a relatively small number of objects or scenes is to be interpreted. The best examples of this situation can

73

EXHIBIT 17

MACHINE VISION VS. HUMAN VISION:
EVALUATION OF PERFORMANCE

PERFORMANCE CRITERIA	MACHINE VISION	HUMAN VISION
RESOLUTION	LIMITED BY PIXEL ARRAY SIZE	HIGH RESOLUTION CAPABILITY
PROCESSING SPEED	FRACTION OF A SECOND PER IMAGE	REAL TIME PROCESSING
DISCRIMINATION	LIMITED TO HIGH CONTRAST IMAGES	VERY SENSITIVE DISCRIMINATION
ACCURACY	ACCURATE FOR PART DISCRIMINATION BASED UPON QUANTITATIVE DIFFERENCES. ACCURACY REMAINS CONSISTENT AT HIGH PRODUCTION VOLUME.	ACCURATE AT DISTINGUISHING QUALITATIVE DIFFERENCES. MAY DECREASE AT HIGH VOLUME.
OPERATING COST	HIGH FOR LOW VOLUME, LOWER THAN HUMAN VISION AT HIGH VOLUME	LOWER THAN MACHINE AT LOW VOLUME
OVERALL:	BEST AT HIGH PRODUCTION VOLUME	BEST AT LOW OR MODERATE PRODUCTION VOLUME

be found in a job shop environment in which craft workers produce one-of-a-kind, hand manufactured items such as furniture or musical instruments. The most suitable applications for machine vision systems are likely to be found in high volume manufacturing environments in which a variety of different categories of parts or products are manufactured, each with readily distinguishable features, and in which parts are presented for visual examination with at least a certain degree of structure.

SUITABLE APPLICATIONS

In general, machine vision systems are suitable for use in three categories of manufacturing applications. First, they can be used for visual inspection of a variety of parts, sub-assemblies, and finished products to insure that certain standards are met. Second, they can be used to identify parts for sorting them into groups. Third, they are suitable for guidance and control applications, such as controlling the motion of a robot manipulator. Examples in each of these three areas are listed in Exhibit 18.

Inspection

The ability of an automated vision system to recognize well-defined patterns and determine if these patterns match those stored in the system's memory makes it ideal for the inspection of parts, assemblies, containers, and labels. Two types of inspection can be performed by vision systems: quantitative and qualitative. Quantitative inspection is the verification that measurable quantities fall within desired ranges of tolerance, such as dimensional measurements or numbers of holes. Qualitative inspection

EXHIBIT 18

EXAMPLES OF CURRENT VISION SYSTEM APPLICATIONS

AREA	SAMPLE APPLICATIONS
INSPECTION	• Measurement of length, width and area
	• Measurement of hole diameter and position
	• Inspection of part profile and contour
	• Crack detection
	• On-line inspection of assemblies
	• Verification of part features
	• Inspection of surface finish
GUIDANCE & CONTROL	• Vision-assisted robot assembly
	• Vision-assisted robot material handling
	• Weld seam tracking
	• Part orientation and alignment systems
	• Determining part position and orientation
	• Monitoring high speed packaging equipment
PART IDENTIFICATION	• Optical character recognition
	• Identification of parts for spray painting
	• Conveyor belt part sording
	• Bin picking
	• Keyboard and display verification

is the verification that certain components or properties are present and in a certain position, such as defects, missing parts, extraneous components, or misaligned parts. The output from a machine vision inspection task is normally a pass/reject evaluation for the object being inspected, although actual measurement data may also be an output for statistical process control and record keeping purposes.

Visual inspection represents one of the last manufacturing areas in which automation techniques have been employed. Most visual inspection is performed manually, either by simple observation or by using a measurement tool, such as an optical comparator. One major advantage of using machine vision systems in place of human inspectors is that they can be used to perform 100% on-line inspection of parts at high speeds, possibly in working environments that are unpleasant for humans. Human workers are subject to fatigue, boredom, and the need for breaks, while machine vision systems can operate with consistent results over long periods of time. As a result, while human inspectors can only expect to achieve an 85-90% rate of accuracy in many situations, machine vision systems can achieve close to a 100% accuracy rate.

The types of objects for which vision systems are being used or considered for use in inspection applications include raw materials, machined parts, assemblies, finished products, containers, labels, and markings. They have been considered for use with parts or products which have very simple geometries as well as those with very complex geometries, such as aerospace body frames or engine castings. Machine vision systems are also being used by almost every manufacturing industry inspecting a wide variety of parts and assemblies, including glass containers and textiles, machined parts, microelectronics and printed circuit boards, stampings and forgings, fasteners and gears, and pharmaceuticals and food products.

The advantage of using machine vision for low volume, complex parts is that it is generally both faster and less error prone than human inspection. A complex part may require hundreds of measurements, which must be performed in a logical sequence to avoid missing any steps. The same qualities which make machine vision suitable for high production volume applications also make it suitable for parts with a large number of features to be inspected.

Inspection tasks generally require the ability to detect or measure certain basic features of parts, such as dimensions or image area. Exhibit 19 shows which vision system capabilities are especially desirable in performing a number of operations. Also shown is the most desirable image interpretation model to use in each application (two- or three-dimensional). Finally, the performance criteria which are especially important are shown for each application.

Inspection tasks are generally more concerned with verification of presence or measurement than with actual recognition of objects. Therefore, the most useful vision system capabilities for inspection applications include the ability to segment images by forming edges and the ability to measure geometric features of these images and segments. Two-dimensional images are generally used to perform these applications. Of the three performance criteria considered here, the most important for visual inspection is the ability to perform the task with high speed.

Visual inspection of all types, including quantitative and qualitative inspection, has been estimated to account for about 10% of the total labor cost of all manufactured durable goods. This high number can be reduced significantly when machine vision is employed. Along with lower cost, the final quality of the product can be increased. A number of major inspection applications for which machine vision systems are potentially best suited are considered in the following sections.

POTENTIAL MACHINE VISION APPLICATIONS AND MOST DESIRABLE VISION SYSTEM CHARACTERISTICS

APPLICATIONS		IMAGE SHAPES	DISTANCE (RANGE)	ORIENTATION	MOTION	SURFACE SHADING	2—DIMENSIONS	3—DIMENSIONS	HIGH RESOLUTION	HIGH SPEED	HIGH DISCRIMINATION
		FEATURE MEASUREMENT CAPABILITIES					IMAGE MODEL		PERFORMANCE		
INSPECTION	DIMENSIONAL ACCURACY	●					●			●	
	HOLE LOCATION & NUMBER	●					●			●	
	COMPONENT VERIFICATION	●		●			●			●	
	COMPONENT DEFECTS	●					●			●	
	SURFACE FLAWS					●	●				●
	SURFACE CONTOUR ACCURACY		●					●	●		●
PART IDENTIFICATION	PART SORTING	●					●			●	
	PALLETIZING	●		●			●			●	
	CHARACTER RECOGNITION	●					●			●	
	INVENTORY MONITORING	●					●			●	
	CONVEYOR PICKING—NO OVERLAP	●		●			●			●	
	CONVEYOR PICKING—OVERLAP	●		●		●	●		●		●
	BIN PICKING	●	●	●		●		●	●		●
GUIDANCE AND CONTROL	SEAM WELD TRACKING		●	●		●		●	●		●
	PART POSITIONING	●	●	●				●	●		
	PROCESSING/MACHINING	●	●	●				●	●		
	FASTENING/ASSEMBLY	●	●	●				●	●		
	COLLISION AVOIDANCE	●	●	●	●			●		●	

Dimensional Accuracy

A wide range of industries and potential applications require that specific dimensional accuracies for parts or finished products be maintained within certain tolerance ranges. Although visual measurement systems, such as optical comparators, can achieve a high degree of accuracy in measuring dimensions, they are generally not suitable for 100% on-line inspection applications. Machine vision systems, however, are ideal for performing 100% inspection of items which are moving at high line speeds or which have features that are difficult to measure. They are suitable for either discrete part measurement or measurement of continuous items, such as strip stock or wire.

Dimensions are typically inspected through the use of image windowing to reduce the data processing requirements. For example, a simple linear edge length measurement might be performed by positioning a long window one pixel in width along the edge. The length of the edge could then be determined by counting the number of pixels in the window and translating to inches or millimeters. The output of such a dimensional measurement process is normally a "pass-fail" signal, which may either be received by a human operator or by an automated manipulator, such as a robot. When a robot is employed, the robot's controller will command that the part be moved either to the next stage of processing or to a rework station. In the case of a continuous process, a signal that the critical dimension being monitored is outside of the tolerance limits may cause the operation to stop, or it may cause the forming machine to automatically alter the process.

An example of a dimensional inspection system from AID, Inc., for inspecting card-edge connectors is shown in Exhibit 20. The system measures the bifurcated gap dimension on the bottom of the connector to the nearest .0001" and measures post lengths relative to the

EXHIBIT 20

INSPECTION OF ELECTRONIC CONNECTORS

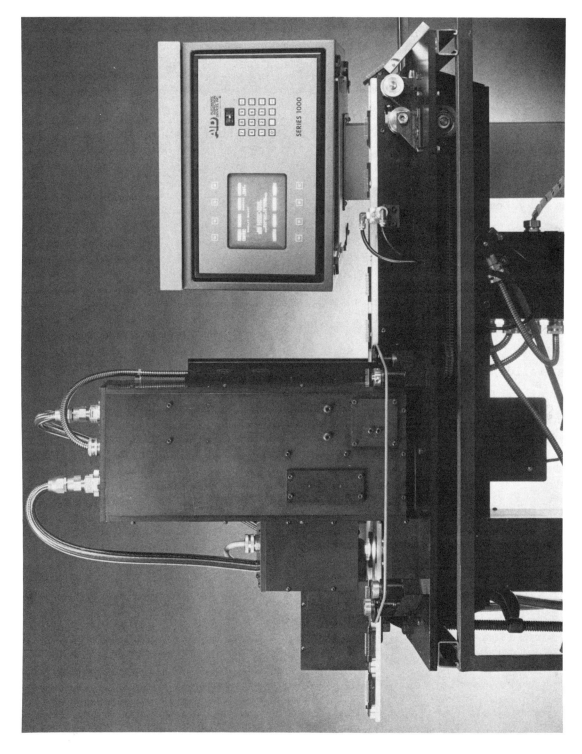

(PHOTO COURTESY OF AUTOMATIC INSPECTION DEVICES)

81

connector base to within .001". The system's extremely high data throughput capability permits each contact gap and post length to be measured from 5 to 10 times each assuring precise inspection.

Overall, the system makes over 3000 individual measurements every second, allowing it to meet production rates of up to 8 connector inches per second or, for example, 240 2-inch connectors per minute. The system's high speed capabilities permit on-line operation at the end of a connector assembly machine to inspect post insertion depth and contact gap spacing.

The system uses multiple vision processing units and three high-resolution CCD linear array cameras, as well as a customized connector transport system.

The inspection system's memory stores set-up parameters for quick operator start-up and rapid changeovers by recalling part numbers from a library of up to 24 files. The system also provides statistical quality data feedback for production and process control functions, including quality trend plots, classified measurement counts, and video-format display.

Hole Location and Number

Dimensional accuracy measurement is a quantitative type of inspection which, if performed by a human inspector, requires the use of some type of a measuring gage. The next application, however, is a semi-qualitative inspection task which requires only limited measurement capability. Machine vision is ideally suited for determining if a well-defined object is in the correct location relative to some other well-defined object. Machined objects typically consist of a wide variety of holes that are drilled, punched, or cut at specified locations on the part. Holes may be in the shape of circular openings, slits, squares, or more complex shapes. Machine vision systems can verify that the correct holes are in the correct locations, and they can perform this operation at very high speeds. For example, vision systems have been used to inspect punched holes in sheet metal applications at rates of up to 2200 holes per minute.

The inspection process typically begins with the formation of a window around the hole being inspected. If the hole is not too close to another hole or to the edge of the workpiece, then only the image of the hole will appear in the window, and the measurement process consists of simply counting pixels. Depending on the needs of the user, a part failure may be defined as any of several situations:

- The hole is the wrong size (measurement of image area).

- The hole is not located correctly (measurement of two or three points along the edge of the hole).

- The hole is missing (counting the white pixels).

- There are extra holes within the window (edge detection or pixel counting).

- A slug was not removed after a punching operation (similar to missing hole).

- The hole is shaped incorrectly (detection of boundary locations).

Hole inspection is a relatively straightforward application for machine vision if the holes extend through the part. It requires only a two-dimensional binary image and the ability to locate edges, create image segments, and analyze basic features. For groups of closely located holes, it may also require the ability to analyze the general organization of an image, such as the positions of holes relative to each other. If the holes do not extend through the part or are occluded in some other way to prevent obtaining a clear silhouette of the hole, then inspection becomes much more difficult. Under these circumstances, special lighting or gray scale image processing may be required to determine the hole perimeter.

Component Verification

A related inspection application is the verification of whether or not a component part in an assembled object is located in the correct position, and, in some cases, whether or not the component is the correct part. In this case, a limited amount of object recognition capability may therefore be required. The most fundamental task in this application is to determine whether or not a component part is even present, as in the case of hole inspection. A part may be a machined part which is joined to another piece, or it may be a separate item which is placed in a container.

A machine vision system can confirm presence by simply scanning the workpiece or sub-assembly and forming a window around the assumed location of the component. A simple pixel counting procedure will confirm presence and, if the shape of the part is easily identifiable, may allow verification that the part is the correct one. If the attached part is of a more complex shape, additional analysis may be required to confirm its identity.

Today's vision systems, however, are primarily used to determine presence and correct position, which are the more important concerns. This means that the orientation of the part may also need to be determined. Vision systems are rarely used for complex verification of parts in three dimensions, when the orientation of the part may alter the nature of the image. However, this is an area in which much developmental work is being performed to create algorithms for three-dimensional image interpretations. In those rare instances where vision systems are currently used for component verification in three dimensions, they are based on either the use of multiple templates representing each of the possible component orientations or complex and costly custom system designs.

The use of a machine vision system for component verification is illustrated in Exhibit 21, which depicts a system for automatically inspecting automotive bearing assemblies. The system, which was installed onto an existing automatic assembly machine, inspects for the presence of bearing components, the presence and volume of grease on the assembly, and the proper seating of mounting bolts. The system inspects 12 assemblies per minute. Prior to installation of the system, inspection was performed manually with an accuracy of only 80 to 85%.

The verification of objects in containers is another example in which vision systems are being used for inspecting components. The best example of this is the inspection of premiums in detergent, snack, cereal, and other containers. The cost of a missing premium can be translated directly into customer dissatisfaction and possibly lost sales.

Another good example of verification of objects in containers is the inspection of pharmaceutical and medical product packages to insure that they include the necessary contents, such as instruction sheets. The display screen from such a vision system is shown in Exhibit 22. This is the Octek InVision system for automated package content verification and inspection at up to speeds of 300 packages per minute.

Component Defects

If the component is present and in the correct position, it may still

EXHIBIT 21

AUTOMATIC BEARING ASSEMBLY INSPECTION

EXHIBIT 22

AUTOMATIC VERIFICATION OF PACKAGE CONTENTS

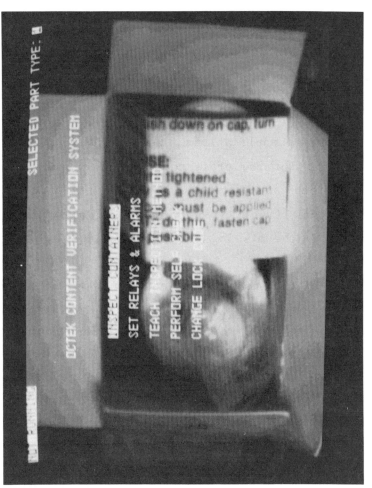

(PHOTO COURTESY OF OCTEK)

be unacceptable because of some defect in its construction. Two types of defects are possible: functional and cosmetic. A functional defect is a physical error, such as a broken part, which can prevent the finished product from performing as intended. A cosmetic defect is a flaw in the appearance of an object which will not interfere with the product's performance but may decrease the product's value as perceived by the user. Examples of cosmetic defects are blemished tires, misaligned product labels, dents or scratches in containers, or character defects on instrument panels.

Although most defects are detected through the use of binary vision systems, gray scale systems are ideal for detecting subtle differences in contrast between various regions on the surface of the parts, which may indicate the presence of defects. For a large number of straightforward applications, two-dimensional binary images are adequate. For example, the presence of a defect on a blow molded plastic bottle, such as an extraneous piece of plastic, is easily identified through its image. Similarly, a broken part can be identified by observing the missing pixels in the image.

Other examples of defect inspection include: inspection of glass tubing for bubbles; label position on bottles; deformations in metal cans; flashing; deterioration of dies; cap seals on bottles; soil on packages; and keyboard character deformations.

Surface Flaws

Component defects refer primarily to physical shape irregularities through breakage or other flaws. But there may also exist flaws on the surface of a part or finished product which do not affect the shape or configuration of the object. These surface flaws may result from defects in a surface finishing process, for example, which causes a surface texture that is either too rough or too smooth. Another surface flaw may be the application of the wrong color to a part. The detection of these surface flaws requires the ability to interpret surface shadings (variations in light intensity) and a high degree of discrimination.

Many vision systems used for inspecting surfaces employ a laser scanner. The laser is directed toward the surface, from which it is reflected to a sensor. The presence of surface flaws, such as an overly rough surface or a series of scratches, will cause the laser to be scattered, with the amount of scattering directly affecting the intensity of the detector signal. The extent of signal variation can be analyzed to infer surface characteristics.

Current examples of this approach include the inspection of hydraulic valve lifter surfaces and the inspection of silicon wafers used in integrated circuits, which must be both flat and clean.

Surface Contour Accuracy

Another important area of surface inspection is the determination that a three-dimensional curved surface has the correct shape. For example, such complex manufactured parts as engine block castings or aircraft frames have very irregular three-dimensional shapes. However, these complex shapes must meet a large number of dimensional tolerance specifications. Manual inspection of these shapes may require several hours for each item. One of the more intriguing machine vision developments today is the use of a vision system for mapping the surface of complex three-dimensional objects.

A good example of this is a system being offered by Robotic Vision Systems Inc. The Automated Component Optical Measurement System (ACOMS) (Exhibit 23) is a three-dimensional optical inspection and measurement system which can greatly reduce the time required to inspect large and complex shapes. The ACOMS was first installed in 1981 and successfully used to reduce inspection time for diesel

EXHIBIT 23

AUTOMATED COMPONENT OPTICAL MEASUREMENT SYSTEM

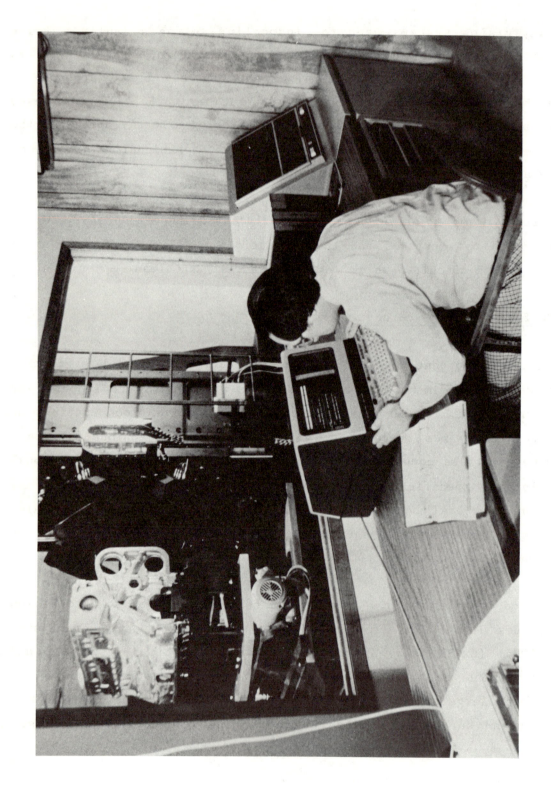

(PHOTO COURTESY OF ROBOTIC VISION SYSTEMS)

engine casting from between 16 and 32 hours to less than one hour. The system uses a laser beam light source and a triangulation algorithm to determine distance to the surface at any given point. The system achieves accuracies in distance measurement to within .010 inches. A set of four fixed sensors scan portions of the surface of the casting until the entire surface is scanned. The casting is then rotated 90° and the process continues. The final result is a three-dimensional computer map of the casting, which is then compared with a blueprint pattern stored in a computer to determine errors in dimensional tolerances. The ACOMS system is presently used to measure some 1250 items for each casting.

Part Identification

The most fundamental use for a machine vision system is the recognition of an object from its image. Inspection deals with the examination of characteristics of objects without necessarily requiring that the objects be identified. In part recognition, however, it is necessary to make a positive identification of an object and then make a decision from that knowledge. Generally, that decision involves some form of a categorization of the object into one of several groups. This categorization can be in the form of information, such as categories of inventories to be monitored, or it can be in a physical form, as in the placement of parts on different conveyor belts, depending on their characteristics.

As seen earlier in Exhibit 19, the process of part identification generally requires strong geometric feature interpretation capabilities, since most manufacturing applications allow part differentiation on the basis of differences in silhouette shapes. As in the inspection applications, processing speed is generally a more important performance requirement than resolution or discrimination ability. The seven basic types of recognition applications considered here often require an interface capability with some form of part handling equipment, such as an industrial robot.

Part Sorting

There are many manufacturing situations which require that a group of parts of varying characteristics be categorized into common groups and sorted. A common example is the process of sorting bolts that have come out of a vibratory bowl. In this case, an image can be formed of each bolt as it enters the sorting station and a simple measurement of image area can be made to categorize each bolt. Several bolts can be examined and sorted each second in this way.

An example of such a sorting station is shown in Exhibit 24. The RoboSorter system from Diffracto can sort and inspect bolts, fastners and similar objects at rates of up to 180 parts per minute. Using a standard inspection program, 11 different parameters are measured and compared to accept/reject limits. Tolerances for up to 24 different fasteners can be stored within the system.

In general, machine vision systems can sort parts on the basis of several characteristics, such as shape, size, labeling, surface markings, color, or other criteria, depending on the nature of the application and the capabilities of the vision system. Once each part has been categorized, it is physically moved to a conveyor belt, bin, cart, or other container by means of a mechanical device with which the vision system can communicate. Such devices as robots, diverters, rams, and other material handling equipment are used.

Palletizing

One of the reasons for sorting parts is to direct the parts to palletizing stations, where they are stacked upon pallets to be

EXHIBIT 24

AUTOMATIC FASTENER INSPECTION SYSTEM

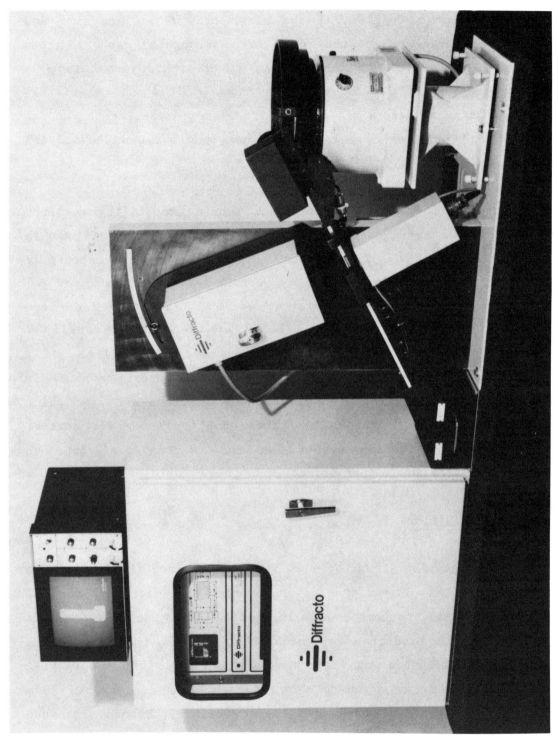

(PHOTO COURTESY OF DIFFRACTO)

stored or transported. Industrial robots are being increasingly used to perform the physical task of palletizing parts or containers. However, robots can only load objects in the systematic geometric patterns required on pallets if the parts are of uniform size and shape and are presented to the robot in a structured manner. When the robot begins assembling the pallet, it creates layers through a preprogrammed set of instructions. Without a feedback capability, the robot cannot determine if any problems arise, such as an incorrectly placed item or a load which has been built up beyond its limits.

Machine vision can provide the feedback sensing capability required for this process by directing the robot to take certain actions in the event of problems. In addition, a vision system is especially suitable for depalletizing operations. When pallets contain several different types of items, the vision system can identify each item (by shape, size, or by reading a label or identifying marking). Along with a determination of the orientation of the item, this information can then be conveyed to a robot (or several robots) in the form of instructions as to which object to grasp and also which orientation should be maintained by the robot's gripper for correct positioning. The vision system can then direct the robot to transport the item to an appropriate conveyor or container.

Character Recognition

In many manufacturing situations, an item can be identified solely on the basis of an identifying alphanumeric character or set of characters. Serial numbers on labels, for example, identify specific batches in which products were manufactured. In the electronics industry, serial numbers on silicon wafers can assist in identifying parts which otherwise would be very difficult to distinguish from each other. Alphanumeric characters may be printed, etched, embossed or inscribed on consumer and industrial products.

Recent developments have provided certain vision systems with the capability of reading these characters and sorting products based upon an interpretation of the characters. One of the best current examples of such a system is the DataMan system produced by Cognex Corporation. The DataMan represents a significant improvement over former optical character recognition systems in that it is capable of reading most characters that are legible to humans. Previous systems required that certain well-defined type styles be used, that a high degree of contrast be present, and that the characters not be deformed in any way. The DataMan system was developed using new algorithms which more accurately simulated the human approach to character recognition. Because certain elements of letters are more significant than others to humans during the recognition process, humans are able to identify characters even when significant portions are missing or deformed. DataMan algorithms are similarly able to infer shapes from incomplete information. As a result, the system can read a wide variety of character styles, even when subject to conditions of severe degradation, distortion, poor lighting, blurring, smudges, or poor surface contrast. An example of the DataMan system reading a laser-etched code on a semiconductor wafer is shown in Exhibit 25.

As more sophisticated image enhancement and data processing algorithms are developed, the use of machine vision for character recognition is likely to grow substantially. Other examples of character reading applications include: hot stamped characters on aircraft wires, dot-matrix printed characters on hot steel slabs; black-on-black embossed serial numbers on rubber tires; stencilled characters on steel billets; and debossed characters on metal nameplates. Software can be developed for nearly any type font, such as OCR-A, OCR-B, gothic, or romans. The vision system supplier typically provides the required software. Typical character reading speeds are currently in the range of 5-15 per second.

EXHIBIT 25

AUTOMATIC READING OF CODES ON SEMICONDUCTOR WAFERS

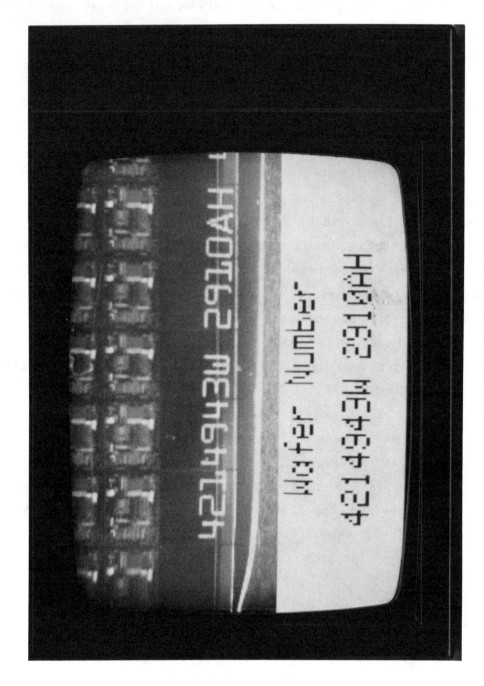

(PHOTO COURTESY OF COGNEX)

Inventory Monitoring

One reason for sorting parts or finished products is to create categories of inventories which can be monitored for control purposes. Vision system part identification capabilities make them compatible with inventory control systems for keeping track of raw material, work-in-process, and finished goods inventories. Vision system interfacing capability allows them to command industrial robots to place sorted parts in inventory storage areas. Inventory level data can then be transmitted to a host computer for use in making inventory control decisions.

Conveyor Picking

In high volume mass production manufacturing environments, workpieces are typically positioned and oriented in a highly precise manner, using costly jigs and fixtures to accommodate the needs of fixed automation. In most situations, however, costly fixturing is not justifiable for small or medium batches, especially when product changes are common. Flexible automation, such as robotics, is designed for use in the relatively unstructured environments of most factories. But flexible automation is limited without the addition of a feedback capability which allows it to locate parts. Machine vision systems have begun to provide this capability during the past several years.

One of the most common situations encountered by flexible automation in batch production is the presentation of parts in a random manner, as on a conveyor belt. This is especially typical after the parts have just been delivered from a process which produces disorder, such as tumbling or vibration. In a typical case, a batch of parts, all the same type, will be presented to a robot in a random distribution along a conveyor belt. The robot must first determine the location of a part and then determine its orientation so that the gripper can be properly aligned to grasp the part. If more than one type of part is included in the batch, the robot must locate a part, determine its orientation, and also identify the part. These functions are provided by the machine vision system.

Early machine vision systems used with robots for conveyor picking were limited in two general ways. First, they were restricted to objects which could be distinguished on the basis of the shape of the object's silhouette. Secondly, they were unable to locate objects which overlapped or touched other objects, except in specialized cases in which special software algorithms could be written to account for certain well-defined types of overlap.

The case of overlapping parts is a more generalized version of the conveyor picking problem. It is complicated by the fact that certain image features, such as area, lose meaning when applied to images which are joined together. A silhouette imaging system may be applied in special cases, such as overlapping circular washers. When two washers overlap, it is not difficult to write a program which identifies the center of each washer and then selects two opposite edge locations for the robot gripper to grasp.

In more complex cases, such as a machined part with an irregular shape, analysis of the overlap may require more sophisticated discrimination capabilities, such as the ability to evaluate surface characteristics or to read surface markings. Various lighting angles can be used to create shadows at the edge of the top part. The occluded portion of the bottom part can be inferred from stored models of the part's shape. If the parts are flat and thin, a two-dimensional capability is likely to be adequate.

The case of three-dimensional parts on a conveyor belt provides another level of complication. One of the best examples of a three-dimensional conveyor line is found in metal casting plants. As castings are discharged from tumble or shotblast cleaning machines, they are scattered at random onto moving conveyors. Inspectors then examine the parts for rejects and sort them into containers. Because of the three-dimensional shape of such objects, as well as the difficulty of providing adequate light contrast on conveyor belts used in casting plants, a structured light approach is required.

The CONSIGHT system developed by General Motors uses structured light and has been used by GM in a metal casting plant in Canada. Two sheets of light are directed toward the conveyor belt, each at a different angle. As a casting appproaches the field of view of an overhead camera, an edge will intersect the plane of one of the light sources. The resulting shadow is detected by the camera and its area is measured. The camera then detects the edge of the top surface and finally the end of the surface, followed by another shadow. As the two light planes form lines across the top of the casting, the camera detects a shift relative to the lines formed on the surface of the conveyor (see Exhibit 26). The vision system software then uses this information to identify the part, determine its dimensions (including height), and calculate orientation and best grasping point for a robot. In the GM casting plant, the system is used with two Cincinnati Milacron robots to sort up to 1200 castings per hour.

Bin Picking

An even more general case of random part orientation is the bin picking problem. The most common form of part presentation is a bin of parts which have no order whatsoever. While a conveyor belt insures a rough form of organization in a two-dimensional plane, a bin is a three-dimensional assortment of parts oriented randomly through space. While human operators have little difficulty selecting and grasping parts from a bin, this is one of the most difficult tasks for a robot to perform.

EXHIBIT 26

GM CONSIGHT SYSTEM USED ON
METAL CASTING CONVEYOR BELT

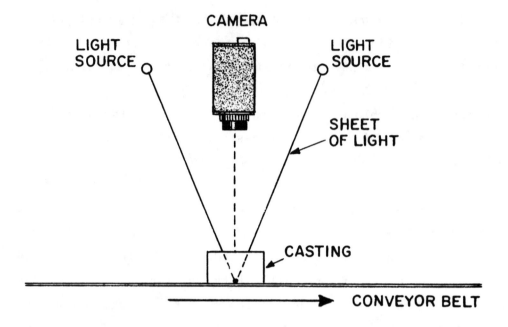

(a) SIDE VIEW, SHOWING PLACEMENT OF LIGHT SOURCES AND CAMERA

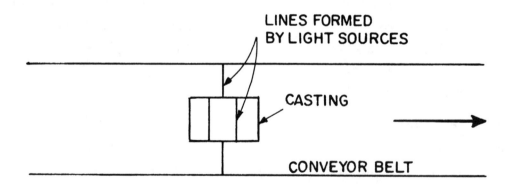

(b) TOP VIEW FROM CAMERA, SHOWING DISPLACEMENT OF LIGHT LINES ON CASTING SURFACE

Machine vision can locate a part, identify orientation, and direct a robot to grasp the part. However, it is not certain that bin picking will become an important application for vision systems. The capabilities required are extremely complex, and alternative mechanical devices are available, such as bowl feeders or shakers, to place parts from a bin onto a conveyor belt.

Guidance and Control

One of the basic limitations of industrial robots in such applications as assembly, machining, welding, or other process oriented operations is that feedback capabilities are limited. In these applications, parts must be continuously monitored and positioned relative to other parts with a high degree of precision. In some applications, such as bolt tightening, a force feedback capability may be required to determine at which point the operation should cease. In many other applications, a vision system can be a powerful tool for controlling production operations when combined with other forms of automated equipment.

As seen earlier in Exhibit 19, these applications tend to require advanced machine vision system capabilities. Because of the need to determine spatial relationships among objects, the ability to measure distance is often important, as well as the ability to measure an object's orientation and geometric shape. In addition, an ideal vision system would allow three-dimensional interpretation of images. Finally, the precise positioning requirements of these tasks means that a high degree of image resolution is desirable.

Weld Seam Tracking

One of the more unpleasant processing tasks for humans is that of welding. As robots are increasingly used to perform continuous welding operations, there is a greater need for an effective seam tracking capability. Vision systems used for this purpose must be capable of maintaining the weld torch, electrode, and arc in the proper positions relative to the weld joint. They must also be capable of detecting weld joint details, such as widths, angles, depths, mismatches, root openings, tack welds, and locations of previous weld passes. Finally, they must be capable of performing these tasks under conditions of smoke, heat, dirt, and operator mistreatment. In general, non-contact sensors are preferred over contact sensors.

A number of robot manufacturers and system vendors now offer special purpose vision equipment for weld seam tracking. The vision sensors for these systems are normally mounted on the end of the robot manipulator arm, near the welding torch (Exhibit 27). These systems are interfaced with the robot's controller and typically use a laser light source and detector to minimize the effects of weld spatter and other complicating factors encountered in such a harsh environment.

Part Positioning

Another logical guidance and control application for machine vision is the ability to direct a part to a precise position so that some operation can be performed on it, such as a machining operation. As in other guidance and control applications, the physical positioning is performed by a flexible automation device, such as a robot. The vision system insures that the part has reached the correct location and is correctly aligned. The advantage of using a vision system is that expensive fixturing can be eliminated. The primary concern here is to achieve a high image resolution so that the position can be measured accurately. In some cases, such as when a part must be positioned so as to touch another part, machine vision may not be precise enough, and a touch sensor may be required.

EXHIBIT 27

AUTOMATIC WELD SEAM TRACKING

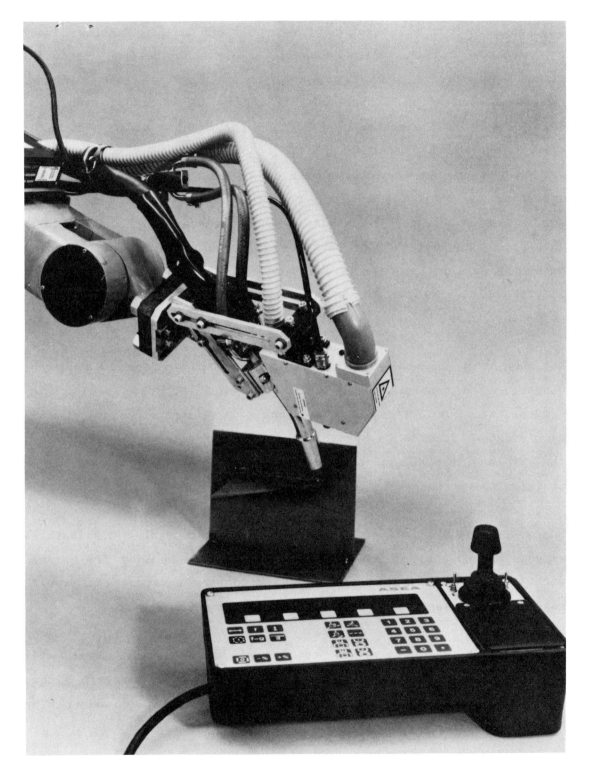

(PHOTO COURTESY OF ASEA)

Processing/Machining

The use of robots for drilling, cutting, deburring, gluing, and other machining or processing applications is limited at present to fairly simple operations which can be programmed off-line. Machine vision can greatly expand these capabilities in applications requiring visual feedback. A machine vision system for example, has been used in conjunction with a robot to drill holes in aircraft structures. This a suitable processing applications for machine vision, since it simply requires that certain points on a surface be located. The vision system can identify edges of the object being processed, determine orientation, and then measure X and Y distances to each hole location. These distances are communicated to a robot, which then drills the holes. The vision system can then inspect the holes after the drilling process is complete. If rivets or bolts are to be inserted in the holes, the system can follow the same procedure to guide the robot to each hole location.

The advantage of using a vision system with a robot is that the vision system can guide the robot to a more accurate position by compensating for errors in the robot's positioning accuracy. In machining or processing operations which are controlled by humans, the vision system can overcome human errors such as incorrect positioning or undetected defects.

The use of machine vision for machining and processing applications extends beyond the subject of robotics. This technology can be used with traditional computer controlled production equipment to provide non-contacting sensory feedback to improve production processes.

For example, machine vision technology was used in a recently installed system for automatically drilling holes in aircraft wings, as shown in Exhibit 28. The 100-foot machine drills two outer wing

104

EXHIBIT 28

VISION CONTROLLED DRILLING

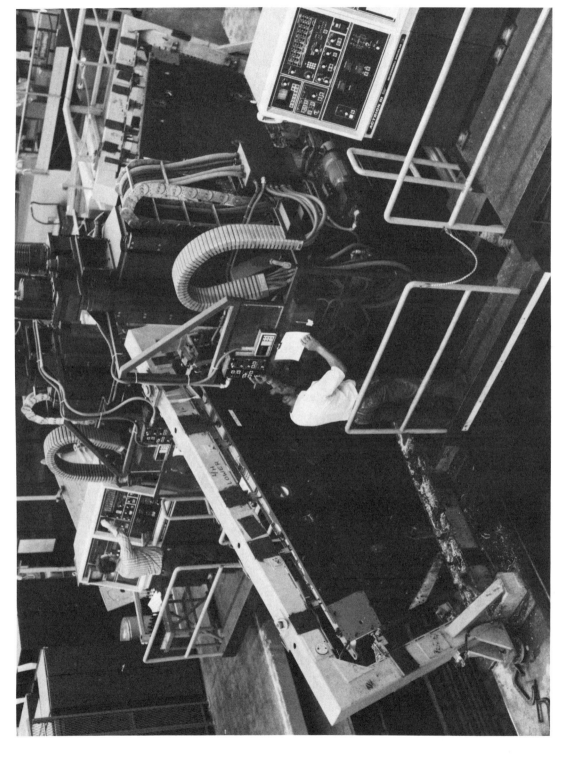

(PHOTO COURTESY OF McDONNELL DOUGLAS)

assemblies and four inner wing assemblies at one time. Drilling is done by four movable, numerically controlled five-axis drill columns. A machine vision system is used to keep the holes within required tolerances -- up to three one-thousandths of an inch. To achieve this precision, the camera scans the wing structure and feeds data to a computer linked to a CAD/CAM system. The computer compares the data with the engineering model contained in the CAD/CAM system and transmits necessary corrections to the drilling machine.

The use of embedded machine vision technology in many types of production equipment should increase dramatically in the next few years.

Fastening/Assembly

One of the areas of greatest interest for flexible automation applications is in the process of joining parts together. Robots are already used for simple assembly operations, such as part insertion. However, more complex assembly operations requiring calculation of spatial relationships and maneuvering of parts must have some type of feedback capability. As the assembly process becomes more complicated, it is increasingly difficult to program the robot's movements correctly. Small errors in manipulator movement along with errors in part fixturing can prevent successful completion of the operation. Vision systems can be used in certain assembly operations to provide feedback control for in-process corrections.

Several companies have developed machine vision systems which operate in conjunction with assembly robots. These systems range from relatively simple part identification or verification equipment to more complex approaches which permit the robots to compensate for variations in part position, orientation or dimension.

A relatively straightforward application of machine vision technology to robot assembly is illustrated in Exhibit 29. In this system, robots are used to assemble and test spark control engine computers for automotive applications. The system includes 18 robots for loading and unloading components, and a computerized vision system for identifying up to 200 different part numbers.

Collision Avoidance

Although not yet available for commercial use, a vision system could be used with a robot or other flexible manufacturing equipment to prevent the manipulator arm from accidentally coming into contact with another piece of equipment, a human worker, or other obstacles. This application requires the capability of sensing and measuring relative motions as well as spatial relationships among objects. In addition, a real-time processing capability would be required in order to make rapid decisions and prevent contact.

Other Applications

As machine vision technology continues to evolve and becomes more widely used within industry, additional applications are beginning to materialize. Many of these applications combine more than one of the previously mentioned functions (inspection, part identification, and guidance and control), while others represent special purpose equipment which has been designed to satisfy a particular need. Still other applications reflect machine vision systems which are embedded in other equipment.

In the future, special purpose systems are likely to represent a large, if not the largest, use of machine vision technology. One of the best examples of this type of system is equipment for inspecting printed circuit boards (Exhibit 30). A number of companies have either developed or are in the process of developing such systems,

EXHIBIT 29

VISION ASSISTED ROBOT ASSEMBLY

(PHOTO COURTESY OF CHRYSLER)

EXHIBIT 30

PRINTED CIRCUIT BOARD INSPECTION SYSTEM

(PHOTO COURTESY OF COGNEX)

which are expected to be widely used by the end of the decade. Similar special purpose equipment is entering the market for inspection of thick film substrates and circuits, surface mounted devices, and photolithographic artwork.

In the embedded technology area, one of the major uses of machine vision is in mask alignment for production of microelectronic dvices. Similarly, vision technology is also becoming widely used for controlling other microelectronic fabrication equipment, such as automatic wire bonding machines for connecting integrated circuits to their cases.

In the future, these two thrusts -- special purpose systems and embedded vision technology -- should result in numerous applications unheard of today.

SELECTION AND IMPLEMENTATION

During the past decade, machine vision technology has moved from the laboratory to the shop floor. Although the technology is still evolving, many practical and cost-effective manufacturing applications exist today, as discussed in the previous sections.

In spite of these success stories, selecting and implementing a machine vision system is not easy, particularly for first time users. Vision technology seldom represents an off-the-shelf solution to a specific problem, and considerable development or applications engineering effort is usually required for a successful application. Furthermore, first time users rarely have the range of skills needed to apply this technology without some type of outside assistance.

To overcome these difficulties, it is important to follow a structured approach to selecting and installing a machine vision system. A three-step approach is recommended: 1) finding applications, 2) system selection, and 3) installation and use. These steps are described in the following sections. The types of factors to be considered in each step are shown in Exhibit 31.

Finding Applications

Once a decision has been made to investigate the use of machine vision technology, the first step is to identify suitable potential applications. This can be done by either a designated person or team within the firm, or with the assistance of outside sources, such as consultants or equipment vendors. Regardless of the team makeup, it is important to select an application which has a very high chance of success, since subsequent use of machine vision within the plant may depend upon the performance of this first application.

In all likelihood, a number of potential applications will be identified in each of the following areas: inspection, part recognition, and guidance and control. It then becomes necessary to briefly evaluate each of the potential applications and select the most suitable, taking into consideration the factors listed in Exhibit 31.

Once the initial application has been chosen, then a preliminary requirements document should be prepared describing the task to be performed by the vision system, operating constraints, expected performance, etc. This document will be the basis for initial discussions with equipment vendors. It is highly likely that the requirements document will undergo revision as these discussions progress.

EXHIBIT 31

FACTORS TO CONSIDER WHEN SELECTING AND IMPLEMENTING MACHINE VISION SYSTEMS

1. **DECISION TO USE MACHINE VISION**

   - **Complexity of the scene to be viewed**
     - Number of objects
     - Lighting Characteristics
     - Degree to which objects touch or overlap
     - Shape of objects (e.g., surfaces)

   - **Degree of similarity among parts**
     - Area of images
     - Dimensions
     - Shapes of images

   - **Degree of structure**
     - Frequency of appearance of parts
     - Location of parts
     - Part orientation
     - Variations in lighting

   - **Speed of operation**
     - Number of parts per second
     - Speed of movement of parts

   - **Accuracy requirement of application**

   - **Economics of machine vision**
     - System cost
     - Payback period

2. **SELECTION OF MACHINE VISION SYSTEM**

   - **Capabilities of each system**
     - Feature measurement capabilities
     - Image analysis capabilities
     - Performance (resolution, speed, discrimination)

   - **Interface/expansion capabilities**
     - Number of input/output options
     - Presence of both communications port and information port
     - State-of-the-art control capability
     - Software upgrade capability
     - User oriented system

3. **INSTALLATION AND IMPLEMENTATION**

   - **Manufacturer applications engineering capability**

   - **User applications engineering capability**

   - **Manufacturer servicing policies**

The subject of economic justification deserves special mention. As with most new technologies, the benefits to be gained are sometimes difficult to determine in advance and vary considerably from application to application. This is certainly true for machine vision systems. Although vision system costs are considered high at present, many users have experienced payback periods ranging from 3 months to 2 years, with 6 months to a year frequently considered to be typical. Benefits normally include reduced inspection labor, higher quality levels and increased product throughput. Costs, on the other hand, often include a system with multiple cameras, special lighting equipment, other special tooling and equipment, and applications engineering. In many cases, the base price of the system may only represent 50% or less of the total investment, depending on the specific installation. Although economic considerations are always important, it should again be emphasized that the initial application should be equally concerned with technical feasibility.

System Selection

Once a decision has been reached to purchase a machine vision system and a clear understanding exists concerning the tasks to be performed by the system, then the next step is to select a vendor, which will be either a system manufacturer or a firm specializing in turnkey system design and installation. Most systems are purchased directly from the manufacturer at present.

As discussed in the next chapter, there are approximately 100 companies currently manufacturing vision systems for industrial applications. Most of these firms are small, relatively young companies which have been formed to produce machine vision systems. The fact that many of the suppliers are small has its advantages and disadvantages. In many cases they can respond quickly to a user's needs and provide more customized services. On the other hand, some of the smaller firms have limited resources and may have difficulty staying in the business over the long term. Thus, care should be taken to select a vendor that can not only provide you with an acceptable vision system but also support after installation, if necessary.

A list of candidate vendors can be compiled by reviewing the information on commercially available systems contained in the next chapter, where the capabilities, cost and suitable applications for over 120 systems are summarized. By comparing this information to the requirements for your specific application, you should be able to compile a list of five or more potential suppliers, which would then be contacted concerning their products and services.

Most users purchase vision systems on a turnkey basis. That is, the supplier is obligated to furnish and install a system, with associated equipment and software, to solve a specific problem. The starting point for the system specification should be the preliminary requirements document developed previously. Undoubtedly, changes will be made to the requirements document as a result of your discussions with the potential vendors.

In many instances it is advisable to arrange for a demonstration of a particular system using your sample parts to help insure that the supplier can solve the problem at hand. This laboratory-style benchmark is likely to uncover some (but not necessary all) major problems if they exist. Depending on the complexity of the demonstration, there may be some cost involved, but this is usually money well spent if it leads to a successful system implementation or eliminates an unsound approach to the problem.

The culmination of the vendor selection process is the signing of a contract or the issuance of a purchase order for the system.

Although most companies have standard policies for the preparation and content of such documents, you should see to it that they include consideration for:

- Performance specifications

- Installation

- Test procedures

- User training

- Warranties and defect correction

- Maintenance and repair parts

In some cases the contract may also specify requirements for testing the system prior to shipment to the plant, special interfaces and ancillary equipment, engineering drawings, and documentation of computer software.

Installation and Use

If all goes well, installation will proceed smoothly and no difficulties will be encountered. Occasionally, however, minor (or major) problems do arise which require correction. Aside from normal mechanical and electrical interfaces, these problems may include:

- Mechanical vibration

- Optical and electrical noise

- Performance drift

- Workpiece variability

- Interference from dust, scrap, fumes, etc.

- Inadequate performance with respect to operating speed and accuracy

Although most of these problems can be prevented through proper applications engineering, many can also be corrected during installation and testing if necessary.

Once the system is on-line, it is important to monitor its performance and benefits. Has the system reduced inspection labor and scrap rates? Do actual results agree with the original projections? What were the "lessons learned" in applying machine vision technology? These are the types of questions that should be answered and reported to management to help foster acceptance and expanded use of this technology in the plant.

CHAPTER 4
VISION SYSTEM INDUSTRY

It is only since the early 1980's that the group of companies which manufacture and market the types of machine vision systems considered in this report have become thought of as a distinct industry. It is an industry which evolved out of vision system research of the 1970's, much of which was pursued for non-industrial purposes. Although machine vision has been technically possible for a number of years, it has become a practical reality only recently due to advances in microelectronics and improvements in image processing capabilities which make industrial applications cost-effective.

This young industry is typical of many new high technology industries. It was initially made up of several small firms, many of which were founded by individuals who had formerly engaged in R&D activities in the field. These pioneers were then joined by a large number of small companies that were formed to capitalize on the emerging machine vision market opportunities. A number of medium and large firms have also entered the market. Today about 100 different companies are marketing complete machine vision systems (as opposed to components) for industrial use. This is at least twice the numer of firms that were competing in this area three years ago.

The industry is changing so fast at the present time that it is difficult to take a snapshot view of it. Image resolution capabilities are improving, processing speeds are increasing, feature analysis capabilities are expanding, image interpretation algorithms are becoming more sophisticated, and applications are increasing rapidly.

Although many changes are taking place in the industry, a critical threshold has been reached. In 1980 or even 1981, the primary marketing challenge for most manufacturers was to educate potential users about the basic concept of machine vision and the technology behind it. Today, these marketing efforts have shifted from education to applications assistance, as an increasing number of companies search for productive ways to use this equipment. The concept of machine vision has reached the stage of being recognized by users and potential users as a legitimate, usable technology. Although many changes in the technology are likely to occur in the future, users will find that existing products are already suitable for many practical manufacturing applications.

At the end of 1984, there were 2,500 vision systems installed in the U.S., representing an annual market of about $60 million. (These figures are based on a recent Tech Tran survey of system vendors and do not include systems assembled from components by end users, nor do they include revenues for components and other services, such as applications engineering.) As discussed in the next chapter in future developments, this installed base should reach nearly 200,000 units during the next decade and annual sales should exceed $1.2 billion by then.

COMMERCIAL VISION SYSTEMS

The machine vision industry is very new, with most manufacturers having entered the market no earlier than 1978. Initially, most commercial vision systems for industrial applications were based on visual image processing research performed at SRI International in the 1970's. The result of this research was the development of a binary image processing technique, known as the SRI approach, which analyzes two-dimensional black and white silhouette images. Many of today's commercial systems still employ this technique or variations of it.

Although the binary SRI approach was probably the key factor leading to the development of practical vision systems, the technique does have some severe limitations. Lighting is critical, and it is difficult to detect surface features or deal with touching or overlapping parts using the technique.

To overcome these difficulties, a number of other image processing approaches have evolved into commercial systems in recent years. This includes, for example, gray scale techniques and the use of structured light. This fairly rapid evolution of image processing techniques is expected to continue during the next several years.

The functions and intended applications of machine vision systems have also evolved along with image processing techniques. Initially, some system vendors attempted to provide "universal" vision systems that could satisfy almost any industrial application. Although these systems were flexible, they were often too complex, difficult to use, expensive and unable to withstand shop floor use. Today, the trend is towards special-purpose systems designed to satisfy the needs of a particular class of applications, such as dimensional inspection, character recognition, robot guidance, and printed circuit board inspection.

The past five years have also brought about changes in vision system hardware. Early systems were usually based in vidicon cameras, general purpose mini-or microcomputers, monitors, and other off-the-shelf hardware. Today, vision systems often employ solid state cameras, special computer architectures and other custom image processing hardware, such as frame grabbers and array processors. Furthermore, system suppliers are offering a wider range of hardware options to match the needs of a particular application.

As a result of these trends, today's vision system purchaser has a much wider range of choices to select from, in terms of technical approach, system design and hardware implementation, than was available only several years ago.

Manufacturers

It is difficult to determine the exact number of companies that currently supply industrial machine vision systems, since the number is increasing regularly and there is no consensus within the industry as to what constitutes a "vision system." Appendix A contains the names and addresses of over 90 vendors marketing systems in the U.S. This excludes camera manufacturers, component suppliers, turnkey system integrators and consultants, which are listed separately in the appendix. The list of system suppliers also excludes a considerable number of manufacturers of vision systems for non-industrial applications, such as medical imaging and processing of satellite image data, and several other firms that are in the product development stage and have requested to be excluded from the list at the present time.

Thus, 100 to 110 companies is a reasonable estimate of the number of industrial machine vision system manufacturers marketing products in the U.S. This is at least twice the number of suppliers competing three years ago. Undoubtedly, this number will continue to grow during the next few years.

Of these 100 suppliers, most are small firms founded within the past three years for the express purpose of marketing industrial vision systems. Others are small to moderate size firms that have diversified into machine vision from related fields, such as robotics or other types of factory equipment or sensors. Still others represent larger firms that have entered the market, particularly in the last year, such as Honeywell, 3M and Eastman Kodak.

Although it is not the purpose of this report to provide market share data, the following companies appear to be the industry leaders in terms of sales: View Engineering, KLA Instruments, General Electric, Diffracto, Automatix, Machine Intelligence Corporation, and Perceptron. Collectively, these seven firms had over 50% of the total 1984 revenue for industrial vision systems. These companies are briefly reviewed in the following sections.

View Engineering

Founded in 1976, View Engineering is one of the oldest and largest suppliers of machine vision systems. Last year, the company was named as one of the fastest growing private companies in the U.S.

View Engineering is one of five vision manufacturers recently invested in by General Motors. GM will supply funds to speed research and development of systems for application to automotive manufacturing processes. GM will purchase up to 20% of View Engineer's common stock and will be represented on their board of directors.

The company manufactures and markets several machine vision systems. The Model 719 is an on-line system for measuring part dimensions and sells for about $24,000. View Engineering also produces the Model 1200 for three-dimensional automatic inspection. The Model 1200 sells for $87,500. The company also makes several pattern recognition systems that are widely used for alignment and sorting in the semiconductor industry, although some observers would not consider these to be true machine vision systems. According to the company, they have over 4,000 systems installed worldwide.

KLA Instruments

KLA Instruments markets inspection systems for microelectronic photomasks and reticles. The company had sales of $43 million in 1983, although a significant portion of these sales would not represent vision systems as defined in this report.

The company has recently introduced its Model 2020 system for automatic wafer inspection which sells for $820,000 and is developing a printed circuit board inspection system.

General Electric

GE has long been a manufacturer of solid state cameras and in 1978 entered the commercial systems market with its Optomation I vision system. GE currently offers several models, including an updated version of the Optomation system, a Scanvision system which uses a linear array camera, and an Alphavision system for character recognition applications. Each of these models has over 200 installations worldwide.

GE was the first -- and for a number of years the only -- large company in the industrial machine vision market. This activity complements its other efforts in the areas of robotics, CAD/CAM and factory automation.

Diffracto

Diffracto was founded in 1973 and is considered by many to be one of the leading vision system manufacturers. Diffracto normally supplies custom designed systems, particularly for automotive and related industries. The company also manufactures special-purpose vision systems for such applications as fastener inspection, gear contour measurement, and non-contact coordinate measurements. Diffracto is also one of several vision suppliers which General Motors invested in last year (1984).

Automatix

Automatix, formed in 1980, views itself as a "robotics systems" company. The company was known primarily as a robot supplier until it entered the machine vision market. Today, the firm offers several vision systems for inspection, robot guidance and control, and weld seam tracking. General Motors is also investing in Automatix with a reported intention of 5% ownership.

Machine Intelligence Corporation

MIC was one of the earlier vision system suppliers. Founded in 1978 by a former SRI employee, MIC produces vision systems which employ image interpretation algorithms based directly on the results of the SRI research. In addition to machine vision systems, the company also offers vision controlled robot welding systems.

Perceptron

Founded in 1981 solely to produce vision systems, Perceptron specializes in custom systems and modular systems to inspect sheet metal stampings, particularly for the automotive industry. Over 20 of its model MV300 three-dimensional non-contacting inspection systems have been installed worldwide.

Other Suppliers

Although the above mentioned seven vendors represent over 50% of the market, a number of other firms should also be mentioned:

- **Adept Technology** - This robotics firm was spun off from Westinghouse's Unimation subsidiary in 1984. They offer two vision systems that can be interfaced with their assembly robots.

- **Advanced Robotics** - This is another robotics firm that offers a three-dimensional, laser based vision system, known as CyroVision, for robotic weld seam tracking.

- **American Robot** - This robot manufacturer entered the vision market in 1984 with a system originally developed in the United Kingdom by Visual Machines Ltd. and Manchester University. They will be marketing vision systems through a new subsidiary, American Industrial Vision Corp., which is partially owned by BMW of West Germany.

- **Analog Devices** - This company entered the machine vision market in 1984 as an expansion of its product line in industrial automation and other signal processing products. Their IVS-100 vision system is a general purpose system and the first to incorporate the new Intel 80286/80287 microprocessors.

- **Applied Intelligent Systems** - AIS has been in the vision market since 1982 and offers several models for a variety of applications. Their systems offer true gray scale processing and are based on "cellular automata" or neighborhood processing image analysis techniques. AIS is another of the firms which General Motors has recently invested in.

- **ASEA** - This well known robot manufacturer offers a fully integrated gray scale vision system for robot guidance and control.

- Autoflex - This company offers several robot vision systems, including a weld seam tracker, a three-dimensional gaging unit, and stand-alone system for three-dimensional gaging and flaw detection for stamped parts.

- Automatic Inspection Devices - AID is a subsidiary of Owens-Illinois created in 1984 to capitalize on Owens-Ilinois' in-house vision system expertise gained from the installation of several hundred systems. AID offers several systems including general-purpose inspection, on-line gaging and package inspection.

- Automation Intelligence - This company was founded in 1983 as a spin-off of Westinghouse's industrial automation operations in Orlando, Florida. In addition to vision systems, the company markets numerical controls for machine tools, robot controls and controls for flexible manufacturing systems.

- Cochlea - This company is unique in that it offers a "vision" system based on ultrasonic technology rather than visible light.

- Cognex - Cognex was formed in 1981 by former researchers at the Massachusetts Institute of Technology. Their initial focus was to develop systems for optical character recognition. In addition to marketing several systems for various character recognition applications. Cognex has recently developed special purpose systems for printed circuit board inspection and package inspection.

- Control Automation - Founded in 1980, Control Automation

specializes in automation for the electronics industry and has two primary product lines: vision systems and assembly robots. In addition to robot vision, they also offer vision systems for printed circuit board inspection and general inspection applications.

- Eaton Corp. - Eaton has been marketing machine vision systems since 1982. It presently offers two off-the-shelf systems, the QR 1000 and the QR 4000. The QR 1000 is a very low cost system, selling for about $5,000.

- Gallaher Enterprises - This firm is headed by the original founder of American Robot. Gallaher offers the GEMINI vision system originally developed by Chesebrough-Pond's.

- GMF Robotics - GMF Robotics is a rapidly growing joint venture between General Motors and Japan's Fujitsu Fanuc. GMF is currently the largest robot vendor in the U.S. The company offers several vision systems for robot guidance, welding and inspection applications. One of the systems is based on hardware provided by International Robomation/Intelligence and designed by the University of Berlin. A laser-based system for weld seam tracking is being developed jointly with Meta Machines Ltd. in the United Kingdom.

- Ham Industries - One of the earliest vision system suppliers, Ham Industries entered the market in 1976. They offer a variety of systems for inspection and pattern recognition which range in price up to $10,000.

- Hitachi America - Hitachi has been actively involved in the development and use of machine vision systems since the early 1970's in Japan. In 1985 they will enter the U.S.

market with a low cost robot guidance system for assembly applications. They will also be marketing a VLSI chip for real-time image processing.

- Honeywell - Honeywell entered the vision market in 1984 with a series of low cost systems for robot guidance, distance measurement and other inspection applications.

- Image Data Systems - IDS was founded in 1983 to develop industrial vision systems. They offer the Imager 3000 system for on-line dimensional inspection, flaw detection and component verification. Later in 1985, IDS is to be acquired by Monitor Labs and will change its name to Monitor Automation.

- Intelledex - This robot manufacturer entered the vision market in 1983 and currently offers the model V200 for $16,000. Intelledex is also developing an improved, high-speed vision system for robotic applications under a recently funded R&D limited partnership.

- International Imaging Systems - I^2S was established in 1969 to manufacture equipment for analyzing photographic images from aircraft. In the 1970's the company directed its efforts towards analysis of images obtained from satellites. It is one of the few machine vision companies that is also active in non-industrial digital image processing areas.

- International Robomation/Intelligence - This robot manufacturer also markets low cost machine vision systems. It also sells one of its systems to GMF Robotics (see above) on an OEM basis. Garrett Corp. owns approximately 30% of IRI.

- <u>Itran</u> - Itran was founded in 1982 for the purpose of manufacturing industrial machine vision systems. Its Model 8000 is a gray scale system designed for shop floor durability and ease of use.

- <u>Key Image Systems</u> - This company manufactures computer-based image recognition systems for sorting, reading, measuring and counting operations. Key Image Systems offers several different models, including their PDQ (Programs Developed Quickly) system and their KR-95 character reader.

- <u>Machine Vision International</u> - MVI (formerly Cyto Systems) provides turnkey vision inspection systems and modules based on a proprietary image flow computer architecture developed by its founder while at the Environmental Research Institute of Michigan (ERIM).

- <u>Object Recognition Systems</u> - ORS manufacturers vision systems for robots and on-line inspection and control applications. The company was formed in the mid-1970's. Included in its product line is the i-bot 1 system for robot bin picking.

- <u>Octek</u> - Octek has been in the machine vision business since 1980. The company markets a number of systems aimed at specific applications, such as package content verification, video monitor inspection, and food inspection.

- <u>Optical Specialties Inc.</u> - This company manufactures measurement and inspection equipment used during the fabrication of semiconductor devices. In particular, it manufactures vision systems for automated wafer inspection.

- Optrotech - This U.S. subsidiary of an Israeli firm manufactures printed circuit board inspection systems. Its Vision 104 model was one of the first commercial systems for this application.

- Pattern Processing Technologies - Founded in 1981, PPT offers hardware-based (as opposed to software or computer-based) machine vision, resulting in faster and easier to use systems.

- Penn Video - Penn Video has been in the machine vision market since the late 1970's through the acquisition of Inspection Technology, Inc. several years ago. Penn Video offers several models and specializes in custom vision systems.

- Photonic Automation - This company manufactures vision systems for the electronics industry for such applications as thick film pattern inspection, hybrid circuits and surface mounted device (SMD) circuits. Reliance Electric has recently invested in the company, which will develop systems for more general factory automation applications.

- Rank Videometrix - This subsidiary of Rank Precision Industries manufactures several vision systems for robotic inspection and other automated inspection applications.

- Robotic Vision Systems - This firm has been producing vision systems since 1981. It manufactures some of the most sophisticated systems available and, in the past, has specialized in large, custom systems and three-dimensional inspection systems employing laser scanners and other advanced techniques.

- Selcom - This U.S. subsidiary of a Swedish firm is best known for its laser-based Optocator non-contact measuring probe and its Selspot motion monitoring and analysis systems.

- Spatial Data Systems - This company has been in image processing since the late-1960's in such areas as radiographic analysis and image enhancement.

- Synthetic Vision Systems - SVS offers machine vision systems based on the Cytocomputer developed at the Environmental Research Institute of Michigan (ERIM). The Cytocomputer is a computer designed specifically for image processing and incorporating a parallel pipeline architecture. SVS markets several systems for image processing research, thick film inspection and other applications. Ford Motor Company has invested in the firm as a minority stockholder.

- Technical Arts - This firm offers a three-dimensional machine vision system based on structured light principles.

- Videk - This unit of Eastman Kodak was formed in 1985 based on Kodak's extensive in-house experience with machine vision. Videk plans to have 100 employees by the end of its first year of operation.

- Vuebotics - Vuebotics was formed in the late-1970's and offers several vision system models. The company recently acquired Copperweld's vision operations.

- 3M Vision Systems - 3M entered the vision market in 1984 based on products developed by British Robotic Systems Ltd.

of the United Kingdom.

It should be kept in mind that there are <u>at least 50 other firms</u> marketing industrial vision systems of one type or another, and a number of other companies poised to enter the market.

Vision System Specifications

Most of the vision systems suppliers discussed in this report offer more than one model. A summary of the 129 most popular models is contained in Exhibit 32. For each model, data is presented concerning when the model was first introduced, the approximate number installed worldwide, the type of system (binary, gray scale or other), system resolution in pixels, typical processing speed, type and maximum number of cameras, components included in a basic system, approximate cost of a basic system, and suitable applications, when this data was available. Most of this information was provided by the system manufacturers during a survey conducted by Tech Tran in late 1984.

Several comments concerning interpretation of the data contained in Exhibit 32 are in order. First, the reader should view the data as approximate. Although steps were taken to help insure the accuracy of the information, some discrepancies exist between survey responses provided by the vendors and published specifications. Tech Tran believes the data is accurate; however, specifications are subject to change and you should check with the manufacturer concerning particular system parameters.

Second, several types of information contained in the chart are highly subjective and very dependent upon specific applications. This is particularly true of processing speed and costs. No standard definition of processing speed exists within the industry, and this

EXHIBIT 32
(Page 1 of 22)

MACHINE VISION SYSTEMS SPECIFICATIONS

COMPANY	ADAPTIVE TECHNOLOGIES	ADAPTIVE TECHNOLOGIES	ADEPT TECHNOLOGY	ADEPT TECHNOLOGY	ADVANCED ROBOTICS	AMERICAN ROBOT
MODEL	ADAPTIVISION/ VISITECH 1000	ADAPTIVISION/ VISITECH 2000	ADEPTVISION AREA	ADEPTVISION LINE	CYROVISION	MAGICEYE VR-1
YEAR INTRODUCED	1984	1984	1984	1984	1984	1984
NUMBER INSTALLED WORLDWIDE	2	1			2	70+
TYPE OF SYSTEM:						
-BINARY	x	x	x	x		
-GRAY SCALE	x	x				x
-OTHER	x	x	x	x	x	
RESOLUTION PIXELS	256 x 256	4,096 x 1	256 x 256	256 x 256	.010 INCHES	256 x 256
TYPICAL SPEED (IMAGES/MINUTE)	7,200	10	6	6	600	120
TYPE OF CAMERA:						
-LINEAR ARRAY	x	x				
-MATRIX ARRAY	x					
-VIDICON					x	x
-OTHER						x
MAXIMUM NO. OF CAMERAS	16	4	2	2	1	4
STANDARD COMPONENTS:						
-CAMERA	x	x	x	x	x	
-LIGHT SOURCE	x	x	x	x	x	
-IMAGE PROCESSOR	x	x	x	x	x	x
-SOFTWARE	x		x	x	x	x
-MONITOR	x	x	x	x		x
-KEYBOARD	x	x				
OPERATOR TRAINING	1 DAY				2 DAYS	
APPLICATIONS ENGINEERING	2 DAYS					
INSTALLATION					x	
-OTHER						
STANDARD SYSTEM COST ($000)	10	20	17	18	50	19.5
SUITABLE APPLICATIONS:						
-VERIFICATION	x					x
-GAUGING	x	x				x
-FLAW DETECTION	x					
-ROBOT GUIDANCE	x	x	x	x	x	x
-MACHINE MONITORING	x					x
-PROCESS CONTROL					x	x
-CHARACTER RECOGNITION	x	x				
-PART SORTING			x	x		
-BIN PICKING						x
-DEVELOPMENT SYSTEM						x
-OTHER						

132

EXHIBIT 32
(Page 2 of 22)

MACHINE VISION SYSTEMS SPECIFICATIONS

COMPANY	AMERICAN ROBOT	ANALOG DEVICES	APPLIED INTELLIGENT SYSTEMS	APPLIED INTELLIGENT SYSTEMS	APPLIED INTELLIGENT SYSTEMS	APPLIED INTELLIGENT SYSTEMS
MODEL	MAGICEYE VM-1	IVS-100	PIXIE 1000	PIX-SCAN	WAFER TRACKER	DEVELOPMENT SYSTEM
YEAR INTRODUCED	1984	1984	1982	1984	1985	1983
NUMBER INSTALLED WORLDWIDE	3	8	100	10	18	10
TYPE OF SYSTEM:						
-BINARY						
-GRAY SCALE	x	256 LEVELS	64 LEVELS	64 LEVELS	64 LEVELS	64 LEVELS
-OTHER						
RESOLUTION PIXELS	512 x 512	512 x 512	256 x 388	256 x 388	256 x 388	256 x 256
TYPICAL SPEED (IMAGES/MINUTE)	120	3600	240	240	720	240
TYPE OF CAMERA:						
-LINEAR ARRAY			x	x		
-MATRIX ARRAY	x	x	x	x	x	x
-VIDICON	x	x	x			
-OTHER						
MAXIMUM NO. OF CAMERAS	8	8	32	8	4	8
STANDARD COMPONENTS:						
-CAMERA		x	x	x	x	x
-LIGHT SOURCE			x	x	x	
-IMAGE PROCESSOR	x	x	x	x	x	x
-SOFTWARE	x	x	x	x	x	x
-MONITOR		x	x	x	x	x
-KEYBOARD		x	x		x	x
-OPERATOR TRAINING			x			
-APPLICATIONS ENGINEERING			x			
-INSTALLATION			x	x	x	x
-OTHER	x	x	x	x	x	x
STANDARD SYSTEM COST ($000)	50	36.5	25	35	18	32
SUITABLE APPLICATIONS:						
-VERIFICATION	x	x	x	x		
-GAUGING	x	x	x	x		
-FLAW DETECTION	x		x	x		
-ROBOT GUIDANCE	x	x	x			
-MACHINE MONITORING	x		x			
-PROCESS CONTROL	x		x			
-CHARACTER RECOGNITION		x	x		x	
-PART SORTING	x		x		x	
-BIN PICKING	x		x			
-DEVELOPMENT SYSTEM						x
-OTHER		x				

133

EXHIBIT 32
(Page 3 of 22)

MACHINE VISION SYSTEMS SPECIFICATIONS

	APPLIED INTELLIGENT SYSTEMS	APPLIED SCANNING TECHNOLOGY	APPLIED SCANNING TECHNOLOGY	ASEA	AUTOFLEX	AUTOFLEX
COMPANY / MODEL	PIXIE-5000	VLS-100	VED-200	ROBOT VISION SYSTEM	SPECTRAVISION 2000	3-D MEASURING SYSTEM
YEAR INTRODUCED	1985			1983	1983	1982
NUMBER INSTALLED WORLDWIDE				16		
TYPE OF SYSTEM:						
-BINARY						
-GRAY SCALE	x			64 LEVELS	64 LEVELS	64 LEVELS
-OTHER		x			x	x
RESOLUTION PIXELS	1024 x 1024	0.1%	480 x 1024	256 x 240		
TYPICAL SPEED (IMAGES/MINUTE)	1800	150	20	300	8	
TYPE OF CAMERA:						
-LINEAR ARRAY	x					
-MATRIX ARRAY	x	x	x	x	x	x
-VIDICON	x	x	x			
-OTHER						
MAXIMUM NO. OF CAMERAS	32	8	8	4		
STANDARD COMPONENTS:						
-CAMERA	x			x	x	x
-LIGHT SOURCE	x				x	
-IMAGE PROCESSOR	x			x	x	x
-SOFTWARE	x			x	x	x
-MONITOR	x			x	x	x
-KEYBOARD				x		
-OPERATOR TRAINING	x				x	x
-APPLICATIONS ENGINEERING	x				x	x
-INSTALLATION	x				x	x
-OTHER	x					ROBOT\INTERFACE
STANDARD SYSTEM COST ($000)	50	40	60	29.5	25	150
SUITABLE APPLICATIONS:						
-VERIFICATION	x		x	x	x	x
-GAUGING	x	x	x	x	x	x
-FLAW DETECTION	x				x	x
-ROBOT GUIDANCE	x		x	x	x	x
-MACHINE MONITORING	x	x	x	x	x	
-PROCESS CONTROL	x	x	x	x	x	x
-CHARACTER RECOGNITION	x			x		
-PART SORTING	x		x	x	x	x
-BIN PICKING	x					
-DEVELOPMENT SYSTEM						
-OTHER			x			

EXHIBIT 32
(Page 4 of 22)

MACHINE VISION SYSTEMS SPECIFICATIONS

COMPANY MODEL	AUTOFLEX WELD SEAM TRACKING	AUTO. INSPEC. DEVICES MODEL 1000	AUTO. INSPEC. DEVICES MODEL 1100	AUTO. INSPEC. DEVICES SERIES 3000	AUTO. INSPEC. DEVICES SERIES 5000	AUTOMATION INTELLIGENCE OPTI-VISION MODEL 200
YEAR INTRODUCED	1984	1984	1984			1984
NUMBER INSTALLED WORLDWIDE		25	40			
TYPE OF SYSTEM:						
-BINARY						x
-GRAY SCALE	x	64 LEVELS	64 LEVELS	256 LEVELS	64 LEVELS	64 LEVELS
-OTHER	x					
RESOLUTION PIXELS		2048 x 1	2048 x 1	100 x 100	380 x 488	480 x 875
TYPICAL SPEED (IMAGES/MINUTE)		250	2000	320	500	200
TYPE OF CAMERA:						
-LINEAR ARRAY		x	x			
-MATRIX ARRAY	x			x		x
-VIDICON						x
-OTHER						x
MAXIMUM NO. OF CAMERAS		16	16			8
STANDARD COMPONENTS:						
-CAMERA	x	x	x			
-LIGHT SOURCE	x	x	x			
-IMAGE PROCESSOR	x	x	x			x
-SOFTWARE	x	x	x			x
-MONITOR		x	x			
-KEYBOARD		x	x			
-OPERATOR TRAINING	x	3 DAYS	3 DAYS			
-APPLICATIONS ENGINEERING	x	5 DAYS	5 DAYS			
-INSTALLATION	x	2 DAYS	2 DAYS			
-OTHER	TORCH&WIRE FEED					
STANDARD SYSTEM COST ($000)	50					25.9
SUITABLE APPLICATIONS:						
-VERIFICATION		x	x	x	x	
-GAUGING		x	x	x	x	
-FLAW DETECTION		x	x	x	x	x
-ROBOT GUIDANCE	x					x
-MACHINE MONITORING		x	x	x	x	
-PROCESS CONTROL		x	x	x	x	
-CHARACTER RECOGNITION						
-PART SORTING		x	x			x
-BIN PICKING		x	x			
-DEVELOPMENT SYSTEM						
-OTHER						

EXHIBIT 32
(Page 5 of 22)

MACHINE VISION SYSTEMS SPECIFICATIONS

COMPANY / MODEL	AUTOMATION SYSTEMS MODEL 615	AUTOMATIX AV3	AUTOMATIX AV4	BEECO VIDEO INSPEC. SYSTEMS	BOICE VISTA	CAMBRIDGE INSTRUMENTS Q-10
YEAR INTRODUCED	1982				1980	
NUMBER INSTALLED WORLDWIDE						
TYPE OF SYSTEM:						
−BINARY					x	
−GRAY SCALE		64 LEVELS	64 LEVELS	64 LEVELS		
−OTHER	x					
RESOLUTION PIXELS	0.0001 IN.	256 x 404	256 x 404	240 x 320	256 x 256	
TYPICAL SPEED (IMAGES/MINUTE)	100	1200	1200		60	
TYPE OF CAMERA:						
−LINEAR ARRAY	x					
−MATRIX ARRAY				x		
−VIDICON				x	x	x
−OTHER						
MAXIMUM NO. OF CAMERAS		16	16		1	
STANDARD COMPONENTS:						
−CAMERA		x	x		x	
−LIGHT SOURCE					x	
−IMAGE PROCESSOR		x	x		x	
−SOFTWARE		x	x		x	
−MONITOR		x	x		x	
−KEYBOARD					x	
−OPERATOR TRAINING		x	x			
−APPLICATIONS ENGINEERING						
−INSTALLATION		2 DAYS	2 DAYS			
−OTHER						
STANDARD SYSTEM COST ($000)		20	32.5		99	
SUITABLE APPLICATIONS:						
−VERIFICATION		x	x	x		
−GAUGING	x	x	x	x	x	
−FLAW DETECTION	x			x		
−ROBOT GUIDANCE		x	x	x		
−MACHINE MONITORING	x			x		
−PROCESS CONTROL	x	x	x	x		
−CHARACTER RECOGNITION						
−PART SORTING		x	x	x		
−BIN PICKING						
−DEVELOPMENT SYSTEM						
−OTHER						

136

EXHIBIT 32
(Page 6 of 22)

MACHINE VISION SYSTEMS SPECIFICATIONS

COMPANY	CAMBRIDGE INSTRUMENTS	COCHLEA	COGNEX	COGNEX	COGNEX	COGNEX
MODEL	Q-920	INSPECTOR GENERAL	CHECKPOINT 5500	CHECKPOINT 1300	CHECKPOINT 1200	CHECKPOINT 1100
YEAR INTRODUCED			1984	1984	1984	1983
NUMBER INSTALLED WORLDWIDE				1	75	100
TYPE OF SYSTEM:						
-BINARY						
-GRAY SCALE		x	x	x	x	x
-OTHER						
RESOLUTION PIXELS		0.003 IN.	.05% FOV	.05% FOV	.05% FOV	576 x 452
TYPICAL SPEED (IMAGES/MINUTE)		300	1	100's	1000's	1000's
TYPE OF CAMERA:						
-LINEAR ARRAY			x	x	x	
-MATRIX ARRAY				x	x	x
-VIDICON	x					x
-OTHER		x				
MAXIMUM NO. OF CAMERAS			MULTIPLE	4	8	8
STANDARD COMPONENTS:						
-CAMERA			x	x	x	x
-LIGHT SOURCE			x	x	x	
-IMAGE PROCESSOR			x	x	x	x
-SOFTWARE			x	x	x	x
-MONITOR			x	x	x	x
-KEYBOARD			x	x	x	x
-OPERATOR TRAINING			5 DAYS	2 DAYS	2 DAYS	2 DAYS
-APPLICATIONS ENGINEERING			x			
-INSTALLATION			5 DAYS	4 DAYS	4 DAYS	4 DAYS
-OTHER						
STANDARD SYSTEM COST ($000)		30	175	36	45	27.5
SUITABLE APPLICATIONS:						
-VERIFICATION		x	x		x	x
-GAUGING		x	x	x	x	
-FLAW DETECTION		x	x	x	x	x
-ROBOT GUIDANCE						x
-MACHINE MONITORING					x	x
-PROCESS CONTROL					x	
-CHARACTER RECOGNITION						
-PART SORTING			x		x	x
-BIN PICKING		x				
-DEVELOPMENT SYSTEM						x
-OTHER						

EXHIBIT 32
(Page 7 of 22)

MACHINE VISION SYSTEMS SPECIFICATIONS

COMPANY	COGNEX	CONTREX	CONTROL AUTOMATION	CONTROL AUTOMATION	CONTROL AUTOMATION	CONTROL AUTOMATION
MODEL	DATAMAN 1100	WAFER VISION 3000	INTERVISION 1000	INTERVISION 2000	INTERSCAN 1000 XT	INTERSCAN 1400
YEAR INTRODUCED	1982					
NUMBER INSTALLED WORLDWIDE	200					
TYPE OF SYSTEM:						
-BINARY	x					
-GRAY SCALE			64 LEVELS	64 LEVELS		
-OTHER						
RESOLUTION PIXELS	576 x 452		128 x 128	320 x 484		
TYPICAL SPEED (IMAGES/MINUTE)	1200		600	750+		
TYPE OF CAMERA:						
-LINEAR ARRAY						
-MATRIX ARRAY	x		x	x		
-VIDICON	x					
-OTHER						
MAXIMUM NO. OF CAMERAS	8		4	64		
STANDARD COMPONENTS:						
-CAMERA	x			x		
-LIGHT SOURCE						
-IMAGE PROCESSOR	x			x		
-SOFTWARE	x			x		
-MONITOR	x			x		
-KEYBOARD	x					
-OPERATOR TRAINING	2 DAYS					
-APPLICATIONS ENGINEERING						
-INSTALLATION	4 DAYS					
-OTHER				x		
STANDARD SYSTEM COST ($000)	30		22.5	22.5	47.5	39.9
SUITABLE APPLICATIONS:						
-VERIFICATION			x	x	PC BOARD INSPC	PC BOARD INSPC
-GAUGING			x			
-FLAW DETECTION		WAFER INSPEC.	x			
-ROBOT GUIDANCE			x			
-MACHINE MONITORING						
-PROCESS CONTROL						
-CHARACTER RECOGNITION	x		x	x		
-PART SORTING						
-BIN PICKING						
-DEVELOPMENT SYSTEM						
-OTHER						

EXHIBIT 32
(Page 8 of 22)

MACHINE VISION SYSTEMS SPECIFICATIONS

COMPANY	CONTROL AUTOMATION	COSMOS IMAGING SYS.	CR TECHNOLOGY	CR TECHNOLOGY	DIFFRACTO	DIFFRACTO
MODEL	INTERSCAN 1500	STRATOS	FMT 240	KT 960	MAXAN	ROBOSORTER
YEAR INTRODUCED		1984				
NUMBER INSTALLED WORLDWIDE						
TYPE OF SYSTEM:						
-BINARY					x	
-GRAY SCALE		256 LEVELS	64 LEVELS			
-OTHER						
RESOLUTION PIXELS		512 x 512	240 x 256		128 x 128	
TYPICAL SPEED (IMAGES/MINUTE)					1200	200
TYPE OF CAMERA:						
-LINEAR ARRAY		x				
-MATRIX ARRAY			x		x	
-VIDICON						
-OTHER						
MAXIMUM NO. OF CAMERAS		2			10	
STANDARD COMPONENTS:						
-CAMERA						
-LIGHT SOURCE						
-IMAGE PROCESSOR		x				
-SOFTWARE		x				
-MONITOR		x				
-KEYBOARD		x				
-OPERATOR TRAINING		x				
-APPLICATIONS ENGINEERING		x				
-INSTALLATION		x				
-OTHER						
STANDARD SYSTEM COST ($000)	47.5	30		19.5		
SUITABLE APPLICATIONS:						
-VERIFICATION	PC BOARD INSPC		DISPLAY TESTER	KEYBOARD INSPC	x	x
-GAUGING	x				x	x
-FLAW DETECTION						
-ROBOT GUIDANCE						
-MACHINE MONITORING					x	x
-PROCESS CONTROL					x	x
-CHARACTER RECOGNITION						
-PART SORTING						x
-BIN PICKING						
-DEVELOPMENT SYSTEM		x				
-OTHER						

EXHIBIT 32
(Page 9 of 22)

MACHINE VISION SYSTEMS SPECIFICATIONS

COMPANY	DIGITAL/ANALOG DESIGN/ASSOC.	DIGITAL/ANALOG DESIGN ASSOC.	EATON	EATON	EIGEN/ OPTIVISION	ELECTR-OPTICAL INFO. SYSTEMS
MODEL	PIPE 1-800	RANGE PROCESS 1-100	QR-1000	QR-4000	IMTRAIN SYSTEM	1100
YEAR INTRODUCED	1985	1982	1982	1984	1983	
NUMBER INSTALLED WORLDWIDE		6	150+	10	75	
TYPE OF SYSTEM:						
-BINARY			x			
-GRAY SCALE	x	x		64 LEVELS	x	16 LEVELS
-OTHER	x	x				
RESOLUTION PIXELS	256 x 256	256 x 256	10 x 32	320 x 240	512 x 512	240 x 256
TYPICAL SPEED (IMAGES/MINUTE)	3600	1800	800	800	1800	
TYPE OF CAMERA:						
-LINEAR ARRAY					x	
-MATRIX ARRAY	x	x	x	x	x	x
-VIDICON	x	x			x	x
-OTHER	x					
MAXIMUM NO. OF CAMERAS	4	1	1	4	1	
STANDARD COMPONENTS:						
-CAMERA		x	x	x		
-LIGHT SOURCE		x	x	x		
-IMAGE PROCESSOR	x	x	x	x	x	x
-SOFTWARE	x	x	x	x	x	
-MONITOR				x		x
-KEYBOARD			x	x		x
-OPERATOR TRAINING					4 DAYS	
-APPLICATIONS ENGINEERING						
-INSTALLATION						
-OTHER					x	
STANDARD SYSTEM COST ($000)	125	11	5	50	25	11
SUITABLE APPLICATIONS:						
-VERIFICATION	x		x	x	x	
-GAUGING					x	
-FLAW DETECTION	x			x	x	
-ROBOT GUIDANCE	x	x			x	
--MACHINE MONITORING			x	x	x	
-PROCESS CONTROL	x				x	
-CHARACTER RECOGNITION	x				x	
-PART SORTING	x	x			x	
-BIN PICKING	x				x	
-DEVELOPMENT SYSTEM						
-OTHER						

EXHIBIT 32
(Page 10 of 22)

MACHINE VISION SYSTEMS SPECIFICATIONS

COMPANY	ELECTR-OPTICAL INFO. SYSTEMS	EVERETT/ CHARLES	GALLAHER ENTERPRISES	GENERAL ELECTRIC	GENERAL ELECTRIC	GENERAL ELECTRIC
MODEL	1200	KRYTERION 250	GEMINI	OPTOMATION	SCANVISION	ALPHAVISION
YEAR INTRODUCED		1984	1975	1984	1984	1983
NUMBER INSTALLED WORLDWIDE			20	200+	200	200+
TYPE OF SYSTEM:						
-BINARY		x		x	x	x
-GRAY SCALE	256 LEVELS		64 LEVELS	x	x	
-OTHER						
RESOLUTION PIXELS	240 x 256	.001 IN.	320 x 240	256 x 256	1000 x 1	32 x 32
TYPICAL SPEED (IMAGES/MINUTE)			650	1800	7500	1080
TYPE OF CAMERA:						
-LINEAR ARRAY					x	
-MATRIX ARRAY	x					x
-VIDICON	x			CID 2505		x
-OTHER						
MAXIMUM NO. OF CAMERAS				8	2	4
STANDARD COMPONENTS:						
-CAMERA						
-LIGHT SOURCE						
-IMAGE PROCESSOR	x			x	x	x
-SOFTWARE				x	x	x
-MONITOR	x					
-KEYBOARD	x					
-OPERATOR TRAINING						
-APPLICATIONS ENGINEERING				x	x	x
-INSTALLATION						
-OTHER				x	x	x
STANDARD SYSTEM COST ($000)	14.6	114	38.5	32	10	17
SUITABLE APPLICATIONS:						
-VERIFICATION			x	x	x	
-GAUGING			x	x	x	
-FLAW DETECTION		SUBSTRATE INSP				
-ROBOT GUIDANCE				x		
-MACHINE MONITORING			x		x	
-PROCESS CONTROL			x	x	x	
-CHARACTER RECOGNITION						x
-PART SORTING				x		
-BIN PICKING				x		
-DEVELOPMENT SYSTEM						
-OTHER						

141

EXHIBIT 32
(Page 11 of 22)

MACHINE VISION SYSTEMS SPECIFICATIONS

COMPANY	GMF ROBOTICS	HAM INDUSTRIES	HAM INDUSTRIES	HAM INDUSTRIES	HAM INDUSTRIES	HONEYWELL VISITRONICS
MODEL	V200	VDS-100	HS-4200	HS-4243	HS-4300	HDS 232
YEAR INTRODUCED	1984	1984	1982	1984	1982	1984
NUMBER INSTALLED WORLDWIDE		10	50	20	100+	100
TYPE OF SYSTEM:						
-BINARY		x	x	x	x	
-GRAY SCALE	256 LEVELS	x	x	x	x	x
-OTHER						
RESOLUTION PIXELS	256 x 256	512 x 192	256 x 192	512 X 172	512 X 192	23 x 1
TYPICAL SPEED (IMAGES/MINUTE)	1200	450	450	450	450	4,000
TYPE OF CAMERA:						
-LINEAR ARRAY	.					x
-MATRIX ARRAY	x	x	x	x	x	
-VIDICON	x	x	x	x	x	
-OTHER		x	x	x	x	
MAXIMUM NO. OF CAMERAS	16	4	16	16	16	1
STANDARD COMPONENTS:						
-CAMERA	x	x	x	x	x	x
-LIGHT SOURCE		x	x	x	x	
-IMAGE PROCESSOR	x	x	x	x	x	
-SOFTWARE	x	x	x	x	x	x
-MONITOR		x	x	x	x	
-KEYBOARD		x	x	x	x	
-OPERATOR TRAINING						
-APPLICATIONS ENGINEERING						
-INSTALLATION						
-OTHER		x				
STANDARD SYSTEM COST ($000)	45	15	1.2	13	12	2
SUITABLE APPLICATIONS:						
-VERIFICATION	x		x	x	x	x
-GAUGING	x			x	x	x
-FLAW DETECTION	x		x	x	x	
-ROBOT GUIDANCE	x					x
-MACHINE MONITORING	x		x	x	x	
-PROCESS CONTROL	x		x	x	x	x
-CHARACTER RECOGNITION						
-PART SORTING	x		x	x	.	x
-BIN PICKING						
-DEVELOPMENT SYSTEM		x				
-OTHER						

142

EXHIBIT 32
(Page 12 of 22)

MACHINE VISION SYSTEMS SPECIFICATIONS

COMPANY	IMAGE DATA SYSTEMS	INTEGRATED AUTOMATION	INTELLEDEX	INT'L IMAGING SYSTEMS	INT'L IMAGING SYSTEMS	INT'L ROBO. INTELLIGENCE
MODEL	IMAGER 3000	TEKNISPEC 1000	V200	ODIN M10	ODIN M20	P256
YEAR INTRODUCED	1983	1984	1983			
NUMBER INSTALLED WORLDWIDE	50					
TYPE OF SYSTEM:						
-BINARY	x		x	x	x	
-GRAY SCALE		64 LEVELS	x	x	x	256 LEVELS
-OTHER				x	x	
RESOLUTION PIXELS	512 x 512	2 x 2048	238 x 256	2048 x 2048	2048 x 2048	256 x 256
TYPICAL SPEED (IMAGES/MINUTE)	400	57 IN.²/SEC.	60			
TYPE OF CAMERA:						
-LINEAR ARRAY		x		x	x	
-MATRIX ARRAY	x		x	x	x	x
-VIDICON	x			x	x	
-OTHER				x	x	
MAXIMUM NO. OF CAMERAS	8		4		8	4
STANDARD COMPONENTS:						
-CAMERA	2		x			
-LIGHT SOURCE			x			
-IMAGE PROCESSOR	x		x	x	x	
-SOFTWARE	x		x		x	
-MONITOR	x		x			
-KEYBOARD	x		x			
-OPERATOR TRAINING	1 DAY					
-APPLICATIONS ENGINEERING						
-INSTALLATION			x			
-OTHER						
STANDARD SYSTEM COST ($000)	20	90	16	17	27	5
SUITABLE APPLICATIONS:						
-VERIFICATION	x	PCB INSPECTION	x	x	x	x
-GAUGING			x	x	x	
-FLAW DETECTION			x	x	x	
-ROBOT GUIDANCE			x	x	x	x
-MACHINE MONITORING	x		x			x
-PROCESS CONTROL	x		x			x
-CHARACTER RECOGNITION			x			
-PART SORTING			x	x	x	x
-BIN PICKING						
-DEVELOPMENT SYSTEM			x		x	
-OTHER			x			

143

EXHIBIT 32
(Page 13 of 22)

MACHINE VISION SYSTEMS SPECIFICATIONS

COMPANY	ITRAN	KEY IMAGE SYSTEMS	KEY IMAGE SYSTEMS	L.N.K.	MACHINE INTELLIGENCE	MACHINE INTELLIGENCE
MODEL	8000	PDQ	KR-95	IRRIS 100	VS-100	DS-100
YEAR INTRODUCED	1984	1983	1980			
NUMBER INSTALLED WORLDWIDE			130			
TYPE OF SYSTEM:						
-BINARY	x	x		x	x	x
-GRAY SCALE	64 LEVELS					
-OTHER			x			
RESOLUTION PIXELS	320 x 240	256 x 256	1000 x 1000	256 x 256	256 x 256	256 x 240
TYPICAL SPEED (IMAGES/MINUTE)	60	300	300	120		
TYPE OF CAMERA:						
-LINEAR ARRAY						x
-MATRIX ARRAY	x	x	x	x		x
-VIDICON	x	x	x	x		x
-OTHER			x			
MAXIMUM NO. OF CAMERAS	8	4		4	4	5
STANDARD COMPONENTS:						
-CAMERA	x	2	2			
-LIGHT SOURCE		x	x			
-IMAGE PROCESSOR	x	x	x	x		
-SOFTWARE	x	x	x	x		
-MONITOR	x		x			
-KEYBOARD		x				
-OPERATOR TRAINING		x	x			
-APPLICATIONS ENGINEERING		x				
-INSTALLATION		x				
-OTHER	x					
STANDARD SYSTEM COST ($000)	50	25	18.9	15		
SUITABLE APPLICATIONS:						
-VERIFICATION	x	x	x	x	x	
-GAUGING	x			x	x	
-FLAW DETECTION	x	x	x	x	x	
-ROBOT GUIDANCE		x		x	x	
-MACHINE MONITORING	x				x	
-PROCESS CONTROL		x				
-CHARACTER RECOGNITION			x			
-PART SORTING		x	x	x	x	
-BIN PICKING		x		x		
-DEVELOPMENT SYSTEM						x
-OTHER						

144

EXHIBIT 32
(Page 14 of 22)

MACHINE VISION SYSTEMS SPECIFICATIONS

COMPANY	MACHINE VISION INT'L	MACHINE VISION INT'L	MACHINE VISION INT'L	MACHINE VISION INT'L	OBJECT RECOG. SYSTEMS	OBJECT RECOG. SYSTEMS
MODEL	GENESIS 2000	SERIES 1000	SERIES 3000	GENESIS 4000	SCANSYSTEM MODEL 100	SCANSYSTEM MODEL 200
YEAR INTRODUCED						
NUMBER INSTALLED WORLDWIDE						
TYPE OF SYSTEM:						
-BINARY						
-GRAY SCALE	x	x	x	x	256 LEVELS	256 LEVELS
-OTHER						
RESOLUTION PIXELS	512 x 512			512 x 512		
TYPICAL SPEED (IMAGES/MINUTE)	1800			1800		
TYPE OF CAMERA:						
-LINEAR ARRAY						
-MATRIX ARRAY	x	x	x	x	x	x
-VIDICON					x	x
-OTHER						
MAXIMUM NO. OF CAMERAS	16	16	16	16		4
STANDARD COMPONENTS:						
-CAMERA					x	x
-LIGHT SOURCE						
-IMAGE PROCESSOR					x	x
-SOFTWARE					x	x
-MONITOR						
-KEYBOARD						
-OPERATOR TRAINING						
-APPLICATIONS ENGINEERING						
-INSTALLATION						
-OTHER						
STANDARD SYSTEM COST ($000)	60	40	50	60	19.7	25
SUITABLE APPLICATIONS:						
-VERIFICATION	x	x	x	x	x	x
-GAUGING	x	x	x	x		
-FLAW DETECTION	x	x	x	x	x	x
-ROBOT GUIDANCE	x	x	x	x		
-MACHINE MONITORING	x	x	x	x	x	x
-PROCESS CONTROL	x	x	x	x		x
-CHARACTER RECOGNITION	x	x	x	x		
-PART SORTING	x	x	x	x		
-BIN PICKING	x		x	x		
-DEVELOPMENT SYSTEM	x			x		x
-OTHER		x	x			

EXHIBIT 32
(Page 15 of 22)

MACHINE VISION SYSTEMS SPECIFICATIONS

COMPANY	OBJECT RECOG. SYSTEMS	OCTEK	OCTEK	OCTEK	OCTEK	OPCON
MODEL	i-BOT 1	INVISION	CONSPECT	SCREENTEST	EYE-Q	IS-10
YEAR INTRODUCED		1984	1984	1984	1983	
NUMBER INSTALLED WORLDWIDE						
TYPE OF SYSTEM:						
-BINARY	x		x		x	
-GRAY SCALE	x	x	x	x	x	x
-OTHER						
RESOLUTION PIXELS	280 x 350	320 x 240	320 x 240	320 x 240	320 x 240	256 x 1
TYPICAL SPEED (IMAGES/MINUTE)	60	280	100	1000	250	600
TYPE OF CAMERA:						
-LINEAR ARRAY						x
-MATRIX ARRAY	x	x	x	x	x	
-VIDICON	x	x			x	
-OTHER						
MAXIMUM NO. OF CAMERAS		2	1	9	2	1
STANDARD COMPONENTS:						
-CAMERA		x	x	x	x	
-LIGHT SOURCE		x	x	x	x	
-IMAGE PROCESSOR		x	x	x	x	
-SOFTWARE		x	x	x	x	
-MONITOR		x	x	x	x	
-KEYBOARD		x	x	x	x	
-OPERATOR TRAINING		x	x	x	x	
-APPLICATIONS ENGINEERING		x	x	x	x	
-INSTALLATION		x	x	x	x	
-OTHER						
STANDARD SYSTEM COST ($000)	25	50	75	55	50	
SUITABLE APPLICATIONS:						
-VERIFICATION		x	x	x		x
-GAUGING			x		x	x
-FLAW DETECTION		x	x	x	x	
-ROBOT GUIDANCE	x					
-MACHINE MONITORING		x				x
-PROCESS CONTROL				x		
-CHARACTER RECOGNITION						
-PART SORTING						
-BIN PICKING	x					
-DEVELOPMENT SYSTEM						
-OTHER						

146

EXHIBIT 32
(Page 16 of 22)

MACHINE VISION SYSTEMS SPECIFICATIONS

COMPANY	OPCON	OPTICAL GAGING PRODUCTS	OPTICAL GAGING PRODUCTS	OPTICAL GAGING PRODUCTS	OPTICAL GAGING PRODUCTS	OPTICAL SPECIALITIES
MODEL	IS-11	QUALIFIER 863	QUALIFIER 866	QUALIFIER 1210	QUALIFIER 2418	MV-PLUS
YEAR INTRODUCED						
NUMBER INSTALLED WORLDWIDE						
TYPE OF SYSTEM:						
-BINARY						
-GRAY SCALE	x	x	x	x	x	
-OTHER						
RESOLUTION PIXELS	1024 x 1	.0001 IN.	.0001 IN.	.00005 IN.	.00005 IN.	.005 microns
TYPICAL SPEED (IMAGES/MINUTE)	120					5
TYPE OF CAMERA:						
-LINEAR ARRAY	x					
-MATRIX ARRAY		x	x	x	x	
-VIDICON						
-OTHER						
MAXIMUM NO. OF CAMERAS	1					
STANDARD COMPONENTS:						
-CAMERA						
-LIGHT SOURCE						
-IMAGE PROCESSOR						
-SOFTWARE						
-MONITOR						
-KEYBOARD						
-OPERATOR TRAINING						
-APPLICATIONS ENGINEERING						
-INSTALLATION						
-OTHER						
STANDARD SYSTEM COST ($000)						144
SUITABLE APPLICATIONS:						
-VERIFICATION	x					
-GAUGING	x	x	x	x	x	
-FLAW DETECTION						x
-ROBOT GUIDANCE						
-MACHINE MONITORING	x					
-PROCESS CONTROL						
-CHARACTER RECOGNITION						
-PART SORTING						
-BIN PICKING						
-DEVELOPMENT SYSTEM						
-OTHER						

147

EXHIBIT 32
(Page 17 of 22)

MACHINE VISION SYSTEMS SPECIFICATIONS

COMPANY	OPTROTECH	PATTERN PROC. TECH.	PATTERN PROC. TECH.	PENN VIDEO	PENN VIDEO	PERCEPTRON
MODEL	VISION 104	APP-90	APP-200	FORESIGHT	VIDOMET II	MV 300
YEAR INTRODUCED	1983	1984	1983	1984	1979	1983
NUMBER INSTALLED WORLDWIDE	60	4	23	8	93	20
TYPE OF SYSTEM:						
-BINARY	x			x	x	x
-GRAY SCALE		x	x	64 LEVELS	x	x
-OTHER					x	x
RESOLUTION PIXELS	2048 x 1	512 x 512	512 x 512	320 x 240	640 x 484	0.1 mm
TYPICAL SPEED (IMAGES/MINUTE)		1000	1000	500	900	60
TYPE OF CAMERA:						
-LINEAR ARRAY	x					
-MATRIX ARRAY		x	x	x	x	x
-VIDICON				x	x	
-OTHER				x	x	
MAXIMUM NO. OF CAMERAS	1	6	16	8	32	144
STANDARD COMPONENTS:						
-CAMERA	x	x	x	x	x	16
-LIGHT SOURCE	x	x	x	x	x	x
-IMAGE PROCESSOR	x	x	x	x	x	x
-SOFTWARE	x	x		x	x	x
-MONITOR	x	x	x	x	x	x
-KEYBOARD	x	x	x	x	x	x
-OPERATOR TRAINING	x	x	x	x	x	
-APPLICATIONS ENGINEERING	x	x	x	x	x	x
-INSTALLATION	x	x	x	x	x	x
-OTHER	x					
STANDARD SYSTEM COST ($000)	235	28.5	42.5	30	38	150
SUITABLE APPLICATIONS:						
-VERIFICATION		x	x	x	x	x
-GAUGING		x	x	x	x	
-FLAW DETECTION	PCB INSPEC.	x	x	x	x	
-ROBOT GUIDANCE	x	x	x			
-MACHINE MONITORING	x	x	x			
-PROCESS CONTROL	x					
-CHARACTER RECOGNITION		x	x		x	x
-PART SORTING		x	x		x	
-BIN PICKING						x
-DEVELOPMENT SYSTEM						
-OTHER						

148

EXHIBIT 32
(Page 18 of 22)

MACHINE VISION SYSTEMS SPECIFICATIONS

COMPANY MODEL	PHOTONIC AUTOMATION V-40	PHOTO RESEARCH PR-830	PROTHON 1000	QUANTEX DS-30A	QUANTEX DS-40	QUANTEX DS-50
YEAR INTRODUCED						
NUMBER INSTALLED WORLDWIDE						
TYPE OF SYSTEM:						
-BINARY						
-GRAY SCALE				x	x	x
-OTHER						
RESOLUTION PIXELS		.001 IN.		512 x 512	512 x 512	512 x 512
TYPICAL SPEED (IMAGES/MINUTE)			1800			
TYPE OF CAMERA:						
-LINEAR ARRAY						
-MATRIX ARRAY						
-VIDICON						
-OTHER						
MAXIMUM NO. OF CAMERAS						
STANDARD COMPONENTS:						
-CAMERA			x			
-LIGHT SOURCE						
-IMAGE PROCESSOR			x			
-SOFTWARE			x			
-MONITOR			x			
-KEYBOARD			x			
-OPERATOR TRAINING						
-APPLICATIONS ENGINEERING						
-INSTALLATION						
-OTHER						
STANDARD SYSTEM COST ($000)	60		10	25	16.5	22
SUITABLE APPLICATIONS:						
-VERIFICATION				x	x	x
-GAUGING						
-FLAW DETECTION	HYBRID INSPEC.	HYBRID INSPEC.		x	x	x
-ROBOT GUIDANCE						
-MACHINE MONITORING						
-PROCESS CONTROL						
-CHARACTER RECOGNITION						
-PART SORTING						
-BIN PICKING						
-DEVELOPMENT SYSTEM				x	x	x
-OTHER						

EXHIBIT 32
(Page 19 of 22)

MACHINE VISION SYSTEMS SPECIFICATIONS

	QUANTEX	QUANTEX	RECOGNITION CONCEPTS	ROBOTIC VISION SYSTEMS	ROBOTIC VISION SYSTEMS	SPATIAL DATA SYSTEMS
COMPANY / MODEL	DS-580	QX-9100	TRAPIX 5500	VOLU SENSOR MODEL 300	ROBO SENSOR MODEL 210	EYECOM II
YEAR INTRODUCED			1980	1985	1981	1984
NUMBER INSTALLED WORLDWIDE			300		13	
TYPE OF SYSTEM:						
-BINARY	x					
-GRAY SCALE		x	x	x		x
-OTHER					x	
RESOLUTION PIXELS		640 x 480	1024 x 1024			640 x 480
TYPICAL SPEED (IMAGES/MINUTE)			1800	3600	1800	2
TYPE OF CAMERA:						
-LINEAR ARRAY			x			
-MATRIX ARRAY		x	x	x	x	x
-VIDICON			x			x
-OTHER		x				
MAXIMUM NO. OF CAMERAS			256	2	2	4
STANDARD COMPONENTS:						
-CAMERA				x	x	x
-LIGHT SOURCE				x	x	x
-IMAGE PROCESSOR		x	x	x	x	x
-SOFTWARE		x	x	x	x	x
-MONITOR		x	x			x
-KEYBOARD		x	x			x
-OPERATOR TRAINING						
-APPLICATIONS ENGINEERING						
-INSTALLATION						x
-OTHER		x				x
STANDARD SYSTEM COST ($000)	35	31.6	40	100+	45	55
SUITABLE APPLICATIONS:						
-VERIFICATION	x	x	x	x	x	
-GAUGING			x	x	x	
-FLAW DETECTION	x	x	x	x		x
-ROBOT GUIDANCE				x	x	
-MACHINE MONITORING				x	x	
-PROCESS CONTROL				x	x	
-CHARACTER RECOGNITION						
-PART SORTING			x	x		
-BIN PICKING				x		
-DEVELOPMENT SYSTEM	x	x	x			
-OTHER						x

150

EXHIBIT 32
(Page 20 of 22)

MACHINE VISION SYSTEMS SPECIFICATIONS

COMPANY / MODEL	SYNTHETIC VISION SYSTEMS TFI SYSTEM	SYNTHETIC VISION SYSTEMS IPR SYSTEM	TECHNICAL ARTS 100X	TESTERION MOP 5000	UNIMATION UNIVISION I	UNIVERSAL DETECTOR OP-EYE
YEAR INTRODUCED	1983	1984				1981
NUMBER INSTALLED WORLDWIDE						110
TYPE OF SYSTEM:						
-BINARY					x	x
-GRAY SCALE	x	x	x			
-OTHER						
RESOLUTION PIXELS	500 x 500	500 x 500	.02% FOV		320 x 244	
TYPICAL SPEED (IMAGES/MINUTE)					120	3000
TYPE OF CAMERA:						
-LINEAR ARRAY					x	
-MATRIX ARRAY			x		x	
-VIDICON					x	
-OTHER					x	x
MAXIMUM NO. OF CAMERAS			8		4	4
STANDARD COMPONENTS:						
-CAMERA	x	x	x	8	x	x
-LIGHT SOURCE	x	x	x			x
-IMAGE PROCESSOR	x	x	x		x	
-SOFTWARE	x	x	x		x	x
-MONITOR	x	x	x		x	
-KEYBOARD	x	x	x			
-OPERATOR TRAINING	x	x	x			
-APPLICATIONS ENGINEERING	x	x	x			
-INSTALLATION	x	x	x			
-OTHER	x	x				
STANDARD SYSTEM COST ($000)	170	80	50+	350	35	4
SUITABLE APPLICATIONS:						
-VERIFICATION	x		x		x	
-GAUGING	x		x		x	x
-FLAW DETECTION	x			PCB INSPEC.	x	
-ROBOT GUIDANCE			x			x
-MACHINE MONITORING			x		x	
-PROCESS CONTROL	x		x			x
-CHARACTER RECOGNITION						
-PART SORTING					x	
-BIN PICKING						
-DEVELOPMENT SYSTEM		x			x	
-OTHER						

151

EXHIBIT 32
(Page 21 of 22)

MACHINE VISION SYSTEMS SPECIFICATIONS

COMPANY	VEKTRONICS	VIEW ENGINEERING	VIEW ENGINEERING	VISION SYSTEM TECHNOLOGIES	VUEBOTICS	VUEBOTICS
MODEL	VEKTORSCOPE	719	1200	HAWK	VUEBOT 200	OPTO-SENSE 3000
YEAR INTRODUCED	1982			1984	1984	1981
NUMBER INSTALLED WORLDWIDE					2	21
TYPE OF SYSTEM:						
-BINARY		x		x	x	x
-GRAY SCALE	x			x		
-OTHER	x					
RESOLUTION PIXELS	.0004 IN.	251 x 244	644 x 483		320 x 244	244 x 248
TYPICAL SPEED (IMAGES/MINUTE)	5	10	10	700	100	8
TYPE OF CAMERA:						
-LINEAR ARRAY						
-MATRIX ARRAY			x	x	x	x
-VIDICON	x	x				
-OTHER	x					
MAXIMUM NO. OF CAMERAS	1	4	4		16	8
STANDARD COMPONENTS:						
-CAMERA	x	x	x	x	x	x
-LIGHT SOURCE	x	x	x			
-IMAGE PROCESSOR	x	x	x	x	x	x
-SOFTWARE	x	x	x	x	x	x
-MONITOR	x	x	x	x		
-KEYBOARD	x		x	x		
-OPERATOR TRAINING	x				x	x
-APPLICATIONS ENGINEERING	x				x	x
-INSTALLATION	x				x	x
-OTHER	x	x	x	x		
STANDARD SYSTEM COST ($000)	80	24	87.5	29.5	12	49
SUITABLE APPLICATIONS:						
-VERIFICATION	x			x	x	
-GAUGING	x	x	x		x	
-FLAW DETECTION	x	x		x	x	x
-ROBOT GUIDANCE	x					
-MACHINE MONITORING				x		
-PROCESS CONTROL						
-CHARACTER RECOGNITION						
-PART SORTING	x					
-BIN PICKING						
-DEVELOPMENT SYSTEM						
-OTHER						

EXHIBIT 32
(Page 22 of 22)

MACHINE VISION SYSTEMS SPECIFICATIONS

COMPANY	VUEBOTICS	3M	3M
MODEL	OPTO-SENSE 2000	DEVELOPMENT SYSTEM	TURN-KEY
YEAR INTRODUCED	1978	1984	1984
NUMBER INSTALLED WORLDWIDE	11		
TYPE OF SYSTEM:			
-BINARY	x		
-GRAY SCALE		256 LEVELS	256 LEVELS
-OTHER			
RESOLUTION PIXELS	244 x 248	512 x 512	512 x 512
TYPICAL SPEED (IMAGES/MINUTE)	8		
TYPE OF CAMERA:			
-LINEAR ARRAY		x	x
-MATRIX ARRAY	x	x	x
-VIDICON		x	x
-OTHER		x	x
MAXIMUM NO. OF CAMERAS	3	2	8
STANDARD COMPONENTS:			
-CAMERA	x	x	
-LIGHT SOURCE			
-IMAGE PROCESSOR	x	x	
-SOFTWARE	x	x	
-MONITOR		x	
-KEYBOARD		x	
-OPERATOR TRAINING	x	x	
-APPLICATIONS ENGINEERING	x		
-INSTALLATION	x	x	
-OTHER			
STANDARD SYSTEM COST ($000)	19	50	
SUITABLE APPLICATIONS:			
-VERIFICATION			x
-GAUGING			x
-FLAW DETECTION	x		x
-ROBOT GUIDANCE			x
-MACHINE MONITORING			x
-PROCESS CONTROL			x
-CHARACTER RECOGNITION			x
-PART SORTING			x
-BIN PICKING			x
-DEVELOPMENT SYSTEM		x	
-OTHER			

153

operating parameter is especially dependent upon a number of application-specific issues, such as part presentation speed, type of inspection required, tolerances, resolution, number of cameras used, number of features being inspected for each part, and whether or not windowing is employed. Although vendors were asked to estimate "typical" processing speeds, this required certain assumptions on their part concerning the application. Thus, the processing speeds shown in Exhibit 32 are, at best, only crude indicators of performance and should be verified (by benchmarking, if possible) before selecting a system for a specific application.

The basic system costs shown in the exhibit range from $1,200 to $350,000, with an average of about $47,000. Clearly, these represent a variety of equipment types, from low-cost systems that may be little more than trainable photodetectors to complex, special-purpose equipment for such applications as printed circuit board inspection. Compounding the problem, however, is the fact that vendors include different equipment and services in their base prices, thereby making direct comparisons between models even more difficult. Components included in the base price for a particular system are shown in the exhibit.

You should also note that very few of the systems are ever sold at the base price. Most installations require additional applications engineering equipment, such as multiple cameras and special tooling or interface hardware. In many cases, these extra charges can add from 25% to 100% or more to the base price for the system.

Lastly, and as mentioned in previous chapters, many vendors take liberties with definitions, such as "gray scale," and in the identification of suitable applications for their equipment. Several of the systems "gray scale" do not have true gray scale image processing capabilities; instead, the camera image is converted to binary for subsequent processing and analysis. Similarly, some vendors believe that their systems are "universal" and are capable of satisfying almost all image processing applications. Although this may be true in some instances, many of the systems are much more suited to particular types of applications. Again, you are encouraged to contact the system vendor for data on specific capabilities and applications.

The 129 systems listed in Exhibit 32 represent more than a four-fold increase in the number of systems contained in Tech Tran's 1983 edition of the report. In addition to this growth in number of systems, several other trends are evident, namely:

- More special purpose systems – In the earlier edition, most of the systems were general purpose, with few specialty applications represented. Today, however, a much larger proprotion of machine vision systems have been designed for specific applications, such as weld seam tracking, printed circuit board inspection, character recognition, sheet metal gauging, etc.

- Greater range of system prices – In 1983, the base cost for vision systems ranged from $15,000 to $75,000, with an average of about $32,000. Although the average cost has risen to $47,000, there are an increased number of systems at both the low and high end, and a much greater range of prices. There are over 15 systems with a base price of $15,000 or less today.

- More gray scale systems – Over 65% of the systems listed in Exhibit 32 have some type of gray scale processing capability, although a number of these systems do not have true gray scale abilities.

- Increased performance – Today's machine vision systems have significantly improved performance in terms of processing speed and resolution compared to systems available several years ago.

- **Expanded capabilities and advanced technology** – Capabilities that were non-existent or very rare several years ago are now emerging in commercial systems. These include, for example, three-dimensional vision systems and color vision capabilities. Today's vision systems also reflect a greater range of technological advances, from the use of laser scanning and structured light to proprietary computer architectures and the application of advanced components such as array processors.

Clearly, today's vision system purchaser has an unprecedented range of equipment and vendors to select from.

VISION SYSTEM USERS

There is no concensus within the industry concerning the number of machine vision systems installed in the U.S. Part of this uncertainty is due to difficulty in defining what constitutes a vision system. The relative youth of the industry is another contributing factor. Notwithstanding these problems, the recent Tech Tran survey of vendors indicates an installed base of about 2,500 at the end of 1984, almost a 50% increase over the previous year. Furthermore, the survey indicated that about 1,800 units should be sold in 1985.

As difficult as it is to estimate annual sales and the installed base, it is even more difficult to gauge market size in terms of sales revenue. Compounding the problem is the fact that considerable revenues are derived from sources other than the sale of systems alone. This would include, for example, additional revenue from applications engineering and components of systems.

The Tech Tran survey indicates that the total industrial machine vision market for 1984 was about $87 million. A breakdown of this market by type of revenue is shown in Exhibit 33, which indicates that about 67% of the market represents revenues from the sale of complete vision systems. This translates into a market of about $58 million in 1984 for complete vision systems. In 1985, sales revenue for the total market and for complete systems should grow to $120 million and $80 million, respectively. This represents an annual growth rate of about 40%.

Industries

Machine vision systems are being used in almost every industry. Although early users of vision systems have historically been large, sophisticated companies, the technology has proven to be effective enough and mature enough so that even medium- and small-sized companies have also begun to purchase this type of equipment.

The Tech Tran vendor survey indicated a distribution of the 1984 sales by industry as shown in Exhibit 34. Not surprisingly, the two largest users were the automotive and electronics industries, which collectively accounted for nearly 60% of all units sold in 1984. The remainder of sales were fairly evenly distributed among the other user industries.

Applications

EXHIBIT 33

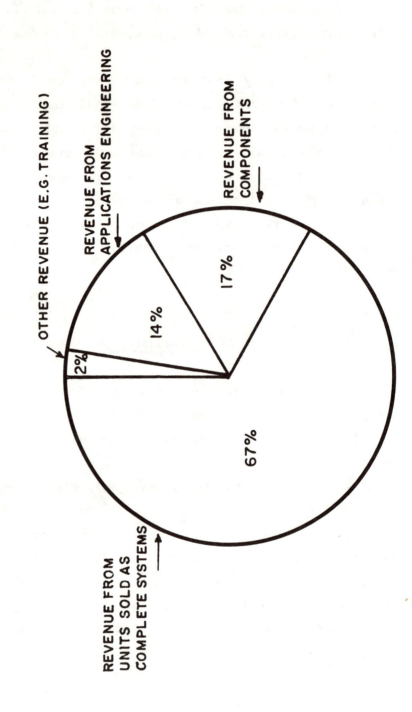

INDUSTRIAL MACHINE VISION MARKET BY TYPE OF REVENUE
(SOURCE : 1984 TECH TRAN SURVEY)

OTHER REVENUE (E.G. TRAINING)

REVENUE FROM
APPLICATIONS ENGINEERING

REVENUE FROM
COMPONENTS

REVENUE FROM
UNITS SOLD AS
COMPLETE SYSTEMS

2%

14%

17%

67%

EXHIBIT 34

INDUSTRIES USING MACHINE VISION SYSTEMS
(Source: 1984 Tech Tran Survey)

INDUSTRY	PORTION OF 1984 SALES (% of Units)*
AUTOMOTIVE	36
PRIMARY METALS	3
LIGHT MFG.—METALS	6
LIGHT MFG.—NON-METALS	8
ELECTRONICS	23
ELECTRICAL EQUIPMENT	5
CONST./AGRI. EQUIPMENT	3
MACHINE TOOLS	5
OTHER HEAVY INDUSTRY	3
AEROSPACE	6

* NOTE: PERCENTAGES DO NOT ADD TO 100 DUE TO ROUNDING

As discussed in Chapter 3, machine vision systems are used in three major types of applications: inspection, guidance and control, and part identification. A breakdown of 1984 sales by these types of applications is shown in Exhibit 35.

The largest application type is inspection, representing nearly 50% of sales in 1984. Within this type, the applications were fairly evenly split between verification, gauging and flaw detection, with gauging being the biggest application segment.

In guidance and control applications, which accounted for 25% of sales in 1984, the largest single application was robot vision. Nearly 16% of all vision systems sold in 1984 were for robot guidance and control. Other applications in this category include machine monitoring and process control, each of which account for about 5% of sales.

Part identification, the smallest category, made up 15% of sales in 1984. This can be broken down into character recognition (7%), part sorting (6%) and bin picking (2%) applications.

A significant number of systems sold in 1984 were for developmental purposes. That is, they were purchased as a laboratory or applications engineering device and were never intended for (or in many cases, capable of) actual shop floor use. These developmental systems accounted for 10% of unit sales in 1984.

The application figures from the latest survey are considerably different than those contained in Tech Tran's earlier report. In the earlier report, inspection represented about 67% of all applications, character recognition 30%, and guidance and control less than 5%. Thus, there has been a major shift in sales emphasis towards guidance and control applications. Additional comments on trends in the

EXHIBIT 35

APPLICATIONS OF MACHINE VISION SYSTEMS
(Source: 1984 Tech Tran Survey)

APPLICATION	PORTION OF 1984 SALES (% of Units)*
INSPECTION	47
GUIDANCE AND CONTROL	25
PART IDENTIFICATION	15
DEVELOPMENT SYSTEMS	10
OTHER	3

marketplace are contained in the next chapter.

DEVELOPMENTAL NEEDS

The potential for machine vision in manufacturing is enormous. Many inspection operations that are presently performed manually could be automated by machine vision systems, resulting in both reduced cost and greater accuracy. Machine vision will also permit both 100% inspection and in-process gauging in many applications that are impractical at present. Some industry observers estimate that over 25% of all future robots will be equipped with machine vision systems for guidance and control. Furthermore, machine vision may represent the key link in flexible manufacturing systems that is required to achieve the goal of the fully automated factory.

Before these changes can occur, however, several basic improvements in the technology of vision systems must be made.

In Chapter 3, the attributes of machine vision systems considered to be the most desirable in several basic manufacturing applications were examined (Exhibit 19). Although many manufacturing operations can accommodate present vision systems because of the simplified, structured nature of the environment, vision systems will not achieve their full potential until these desirable attributes are available in standard commercial vision systems.

At the present time, there are six key issues which must be addressed by vision system developers. Each of these issues, discussed below, represents a basic limitation of commercial vision systems:

● <u>Limited 3-D interpretation</u> - Most commercial vision systems today are two-dimensional. That is, they make conclusions about objects from data which is essentially two-dimensional in nature. In many manufacturing situations, an outline of an object's shape is sufficient to identify it or to determine whether an inspection standard has been achieved. However, in many other operations, such as the inspection of castings, this information is not enough. Many more sophisticated operations could be performed with vision systems if an object's three-dimensional shape could be inferred from an image or a series of images. To accomplish this, vision system suppliers will need to incorporate more sophisticated data interpretation algorithms along with improved system performance (resolution, speed, and discrimination).

● <u>Limited interpretation of surfaces</u> - Complex surface configurations on objects, such as textures, shadows, and overlapping parts, are difficult for present vision systems to interpret. Improved gray scale image formation capabilities have helped somewhat, but vision systems are extremely limited in their ability to analyze the large amounts of data provided by gray scale image formation. The ability to accurately interpret light intensity variations over the surface of an object, which is so fundamental to human vision, must be refined if vision systems are to be used for such applications as object recognition or inspection from surface characteristics.

● <u>Need for structured environment</u> - Although vision systems, being a form of flexible automation, should be able to eliminate the need for elaborate jigs and fixtures, they still require a relatively orderly environment in most current applications. Vision systems have difficulty dealing with overlapping or touching parts, and so workpieces must be presented one at a time to the system. Ideally, a vision system should be able to examine parts as humans do, by studying key features no matter how the part is oriented and even if some portions of parts are occluded by other overlapping parts.

- Long processing time – There are limits on the speed of the operation in which a vision system can be used. Today, only a limited number of "real-time" (30 images per second) systems have begun to appear on the market. However, most real-time systems are used for simple applications rather than more complex tasks. There is generally a tradeoff between the processing time required and the degree of complexity of a processing cycle. An ideal vision system would be capable of performing complex three-dimensional analyses of objects, including surface features, in real time.

- High cost – Although payback periods for vision systems are generally good (one year or less for some applications), the basic purchase price of many systems is still too high to promote widespread use of this technology within industry.

- Excessive applications engineering – It is still nearly impossible to purchase an off-the-shelf vision system and apply it without considerable assistance from a vendor, consultant or in-house engineering staff. Part of this is due to the complexity of real-world applications. Other factors include limitations of current equipment and lack of trained personnel within user organizations. Application engineering cost and risk, and a shortage of trained technical personnel are major barriers to widespread use of industrial vision systems.

All six of these fundamental issues need to be addressed by manufacturers and researchers during the next few years. Many organizations are already attempting to resolve them through such developments as improved computer hardware or improved software algorithms. However, much work remains to be performed in order to develop truly effective vision systems which are available at a reasonable price.

The solution to these problems is likely to emerge from several important developments which are expected to occur during the next decade in three fundamental areas: the technology of machine vision systems, the applications in which they are used, and the nature of the industry which supplies these systems. These developments are addressed in the next chapter.

CHAPTER 5
FUTURE OUTLOOK

Machine vision has become widely recognized as one of the more important new and emerging manufacturing technologies. The need for machine vision systems is becoming well established, and users are increasingly turning to machine vision to solve production problems.

Even if no further improvements are made in machine vision systems, the number of systems in use would continue to grow at a high rate. Machine vision systems have just begun to be used in applications which they are capable of performing.

However, machine vision systems are not likely to remain unchanged. Many developmental programs are underway, both in private industry as well as in universities and other research organizations, to develop advanced vision systems that are not subject to the limitations discussed in the last chapter.

CURRENT DEVELOPMENTAL PROGRAMS

In general, research organizations (university, government, and private) tend to concentrate on the development of advanced technological capabilities of machine vision systems, such as the ability to infer three-dimensional shapes from images or the ability to interpret complex surface light intensity patterns. Vision system manufacturers, on the other hand, normally concentrate on improvements which may have a more direct impact on manufacturing applications, such as the ability to operate in a less structured environment, the ability to achieve real-time image processing, and reductions in cost.

Vision sensing research is an area of intense interest at university, government, and independent research organizations. A recent survey indicated, for example, that nearly half of the total robotics research budget at organizations performing robotics research was devoted to the development of improved robot sensing capabilities, primarily in the vision area. A list of some of the more prominent research organizations involved in machine vision systems in the U.S. is shown in Exhibit 36. The addresses of these and other research organizations are contained in Appendix A.

Most of these organizations have been committed to machine vision research for a number of years. SRI International, for example, is one of the best known and most active. They developed some of the earliest practical algorithms for binary image analysis, which are used extensively by a number of firms today. Stanford, MIT, Carnegie-Mellon, and the Environmental Research Institute of Michigan have also been involved in extensive machine vision research for a long period of time.

Each of these organizations, and many others in the U.S., Europe and Japan, are currently pursuing a wide range of vision research topics, from three-dimensional image processing to improved robot vision. Although a complete listing of these research activities is beyond the scope of this report, a number of major thrust areas are highlighted later in this chapter.

Of course, vision system manufacturers are also pursuing research and development programs. However, these activities are often directed towards solving specific problems or developing special purpose systems. System vendors do not normally publicize these R&D activities until a commercial product is nearly available or a

EXHIBIT 36

SOME RESEARCH ORGANIZATIONS INVOLVED
IN MACHINE VISION RESEARCH IN THE U.S.

- UNIVERSITIES
    - CARNEGIE-MELLON UNIVERSITY
    - MASSACHUSETTS INSTITUTE OF TECHNOLOGY
    - UNIVERSITY OF MARYLAND
    - ST ANFORD UNIVERSITY
    - UNIVERSITY OF RHODE ISLAND
    - UNIVERSITY SOUTHERN CALIFORNIA
    - UNIVERSITY OF ILLINOIS
    - UNIVERSITY OF MICHIGAN
    - UNIVERSITY OF TENNESSEE
    - PURDUE UNIVERSITY
    - RENSSELAER POLYTECHNIC INSTITUTE
    - VIRGINIA POLYTECHNIC UNIVERSITY

- RESEARCH INSTITUTES
    - SRI INTERNATIONAL
    - ENVIRONMENTAL RESEARCH INSTITUTE OF MICHIGAN
    - JET PROPULSION LABORATORY
    - CHARLES STARK DRAPER LABORATORY

- GOVERNMENT AGENCIES AND LABORATORIES
    - NATIONAL BUREAU OF STANDARDS
    - NATIONAL SCIENCE FOUNDATION
    - DEFENSE ADVANCED RESEARCH PROJECTS AGENCY
    - U.S. AIR FORCE
    - U.S. NAVY
    - NATIONAL AERONAUTICS AND SPACE ADMINISTRATION

successful application has been achieved.

In addition to research organizations and machine vision system manufacturers, a number of other firms are actively developing new vision systems, as listed in Exhibit 37. The companies normally develop vision systems for their own in-house use or to maintain a familiarity with the technology for other reasons, such as subsequent market entry. At least one of these firms, Owens-Illinois, has several hundred vision systems of its own design installed in its plants.

Lastly, another group comprising a large number of companies is also conducting research efforts that will lead to improved vision systems. These companies are the camera manufacturers and vision system component vendors. A number of these firms are listed in Appendix A. Developments in such areas as array processors, semi-custom microelectronic devices, frame grabbers, high-speed, analog to digital converters, microprocessors, memory devices, and improved cameras have a direct impact on vision system design and performance.

FUTURE TECHNOLOGY AND PRODUCTS

The time appears to be ripe for the machine vision industry. It has already begun the major growth phase of its development. The product has been defined, applications have been developed, and the initial technology is sufficiently advanced to meet the needs of these applications. Further, a core group of suppliers of machine vision systems is now in place. User education has reached a stage at which potential purchasers are no longer asking what the concept of machine vision is, but rather in what specific applications machine vision can be used and how it can be implemented. Future usage of machine vision is almost certain to grow substantially. Even with no further

EXHIBIT 37

SOME NON-COMMERICAL DEVELOPERS
OF VISION SYSTEMS

—GENERAL MOTORS
—AT&T
—IBM
—OWENS-ILLINOIS
—CHRYSLER
—TEXAS INSTRUMENTS
—ROCKWELL INTERNATIONAL
—HUGHES AIRCRAFT
—LOCKHEED
—MARTIN MARIETTA
—McDONNELL-DOUGLAS
—CHESEBROUGH-POND'S
—WESTINGHOUSE
—NORTHRUP
—BOEING
—GOULD
—FMC
—TRW
—XEROX

improvements in vision system technology, a large market would exist for present vision system products. However, as discussed in the previous section, many developmental efforts are now underway, and it is likely that several significant results of these programs will come during the next few years.

Each benefit which results from these programs is likely to have an impact on one or more of the six basic issues discussed earlier. During the next few years, it can be expected that three-dimensional interpretation capabilities will improve significantly, as will the ability to analyze complex surface patterns. Vision systems will be able to operate in much less structured environments than today. Processing speeds should approach real time, and vision system prices should decline. Lastly, vision systems should become much easier to use and interface with other production equipment.

These trends are likely to result from several anticipated developments:

- Improved camera resolution – As solid state cameras with arrays of 512x512 or even 1024x1024 pixels are used, image resolution will improve. As a result, the ability of vision systems to sense small features on the surface of objects should improve.

- Ability to sense color – A few developmental vision systems are already available to sense color. The addition of this capability to commercial vision systems would allow the measurement of one more feature in identifying objects. It would also provide a greater degree of discrimination in analyzing surfaces.

- Effective range sensing – This is a prerequisite for three-dimensional interpretation and certain types of robot vision. Based upon research such as that being performed on binocular vision, it is likely that a range sensing capability will become a standard feature of commercial vision systems within a few years.

- Ability to detect overlap – This capability will improve the ability of vision systems to interpret surfaces and three-dimensional objects. It will also provide a greater degree of flexibility for vision systems. There will no longer be a need to insure that moving parts on a conveyor are not touching or overlapping, which will reduce the amount of structure required.

- Improved gray scale algorithms – As vision system hardware becomes capable of forming more complex images, the software algorithms for interpreting these images will improve, including the ability to infer shape from changes in light intensity over an image.

- Robot wrist mounted vision system – Based upon work being performed at a number of organizations, it is likely that an effective wrist mounted vision system will be available within the next few years. Mounting the camera on the robot's wrist provides the advantage of greatly reducing the degree of structure required during such operations as robot-controlled welding, assembly, or processing.

- Motion sensing capability – There are two elements being developed here. First is the ability of a vision system to create and analyze an image of a moving object. This requires the ability to "freeze" each frame without blurring for analysis by the computer. Second is the more complex problem of determining the direction of motion of an object and even the magnitude of the velocity. This capability will be valuable in such applications as collision avoidance or tracking moving parts.

- **Parallel processing of whole image** – One of the most promising methods of approaching a real-time processing capability is the use of a parallel processing architecture. Several systems on the market today offer this type of architecture. This approach is likely to be used more extensively in the future.

- **Standardized software algorithms** – Although some standard vision system application algorithms are available, most programs for current manufacturing applications are custom designed. It is likely that standard programs will become increasingly available for standard applications. In addition, programming languages will continue to become more user-oriented.

- **Computers developed for vision systems** – Most vision systems today use standard off-the-shelf computers, which tends to limit their data analysis capabilities. In the future, especially as sales volumes increase, it is likely that computers will be designed specifically for dedicated use with a vision system. This will reduce processing times and also help to reduce system prices. Several systems have been developed lately with type type of custom computer architecture.

- **Hard-wired vision systems** – To overcome the problem of processing speed, some researchers have suggested the use of hard-wired circuitry rather than microprocessor based systems. This should significantly speed up image processing times, but could result in less system flexibility and limited capabilities. At least one firm now offers a hard-wired vision system.

- Special-purpose systems - As discussed previously, there is a growing trend towards special- rather than general-purpose vision systems. This permits the system developer to take advantage of prior knowledge concerning the application and only provide the features and capabilities required, resulting in more cost effective systems. A number of vendors have already begun to offer special-purpose systems for such applications as weld seam tracking, robot vision and printed circuit board inspection.

- Integration with other systems - One of the major problems with today's vision systems is the difficulty in interfacing them with other types of equipment and systems. A number of companies and research organizations are attacking this problem, particularly with respect to special-purpose vision systems.

- Optical computing - It is possible to perform image processing using purely optical techniques, as opposed to the traditional approach of converting an image into an electrical signal and analyzing this symbolic representation of the image. In the optical domain, processing steps like computation of Fourier transforms take place almost instantaneously. Although optical computing techniques offer considerable promise, it will take a number of years before they become a practical reality.

- Custom microelectronic devices - As the sales volume for vision systems continues to grow, it will become increasingly feasible to implement portions of the system design in custom microelectronic circuits. This will be particularly true for low level image processing functions, such as histogram calculations, convolutions, and edge detectors. Such chips should be available within the next few years.

- **Novel sensor configurations** - A number of researchers are working on unique vision sensors to improve overall performance. This includes novel sensor configurations, such as annular arrangements of detector elements, as well as other camera concepts, like multiple spectral detectors which sense energy in more than one portion of the electromagnetic spectrum.

- **Visual servoing** - Several researchers are studying the use of vision systems as an integral feedback component in a motion control system, such as a robot vision system for positioning the manipulator arm. Although vision systems are currently used for robot guidance and control, this is usually accomplished outside the control loop. In visual servoing, on the other hand, the vision system would serve as a position sensing device or error measurement component on a real-time basis.

These developmental thrusts cover a wide range of approaches and technology, which vary considerably in terms of their practicality and importance. This involves two questions: Which of these developments will be most significant? And, how soon will these developments become commercially feasible?

In order to answer these questions, Tech Tran conducted a survey of approximately 100 vision system manufacturers. The respondents were asked to rank each development area in terms of its importance and feasibility. The results of this ranking are illustrated in Exhibit 38.

EXHIBIT 38

IMPORTANCE AND FEASIBILITY OF ANTICIPATED DEVELOPMENTS

(Source: 1984 Tech Tran Survey)

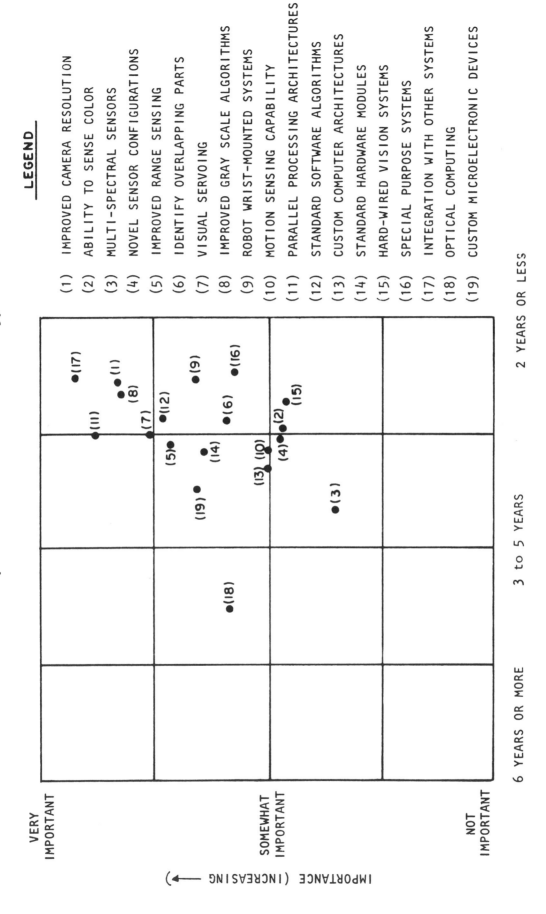

LEGEND

(1) IMPROVED CAMERA RESOLUTION
(2) ABILITY TO SENSE COLOR
(3) MULTI-SPECTRAL SENSORS
(4) NOVEL SENSOR CONFIGURATIONS
(5) IMPROVED RANGE SENSING
(6) IDENTIFY OVERLAPPING PARTS
(7) VISUAL SERVOING
(8) IMPROVED GRAY SCALE ALGORITHMS
(9) ROBOT WRIST-MOUNTED SYSTEMS
(10) MOTION SENSING CAPABILITY
(11) PARALLEL PROCESSING ARCHITECTURES
(12) STANDARD SOFTWARE ALGORITHMS
(13) CUSTOM COMPUTER ARCHITECTURES
(14) STANDARD HARDWARE MODULES
(15) HARD-WIRED VISION SYSTEMS
(16) SPECIAL PURPOSE SYSTEMS
(17) INTEGRATION WITH OTHER SYSTEMS
(18) OPTICAL COMPUTING
(19) CUSTOM MICROELECTRONIC DEVICES

177

Although there was considerable variation in the vendor responses, the survey did indicate that several developments were much more important and feasible than others. In terms of importance, the highest ranking developments were: integration with other systems, parallel processing architectures, improved camera resolution, improved gray scale algorithms, and visual servoing. The least important developments were: multi-spectral sensors, hard-wired vision systems, the ability to sense color, and novel sensor configurations. From the standpoint of feasibility, the most feasible were: special-purpose systems, robot wrist-mounted systems, integration with other systems, and improved camera resolution. The least feasible were: optical computing, multi-spectral sensors, custom microelectronic devices, and custom computer architectures. Interestingly, the respondents indicated that most, if not all of the developments are feasible. That is, they could become commercially available in five years or less. Most are feasible within the next two to three years.

Of primary importance are those developments which are both important and feasible, since these are the ones that are likely to have the greatest near-term impact. These are the developments contained in the upper right hand box in Exhibit 38. These significant developments include: integration with other systems, parallel processing architectures, improved camera resolution, improved gray scale algorithms, and visual servoing.

MARKET TRENDS

As discussed earlier, developing reliable data on the size and other characteristics of the machine vision market is difficult because of the relative youth of the industry, the rapid rate of change taking place and the problems inherent in drawing boundaries around a poorly defined subject. These difficulties notwithstanding, this section addresses a number of fundamental issues relative to market size, composition and trends affecting the machine vision industry. Much of the quantitative data contained here is based on the vendor survey Tech Tran conducted in late 1984.

According to the survey, there were about 2,500 machine vision systems in use in the U.S. at the end of 1984. New installations are proceeding at a rate of approximately 1,200 to 1,800 per year. As illustrated in Exhibit 39, sales of complete units is projected to climb to over 60,000 units per year by 1994, representing a compound annual growth rate of about 50%. This would result in an installed base of nearly 200,000 systems by the mid-1990's.

These growth estimates are entirely reasonable in light of several other statistics. In the 1980 census, for example, it was estimated that there are about 925,000 factory workers involved in inspection, testing, checking and similar occupations, which is about 7% of the total factory workers. Several industry observers have estimated that up to 50% of these inspection workers could eventually be replaced by machine vision systems, which would indicate a potential market of about 450,000 units for this application alone. Similarly, robot vision represents a significant portion of the market. About 25% of robots installed during the next decade are expected to have a vision system as part of the installation. The estimated installed base of robots by 1994 is about 300,000 units, which would represent another 75,000 machine vision systems. If we add to these figures the likely vision system applications for machine monitoring, part sorting and other non-inspection and non-robotic uses, then the overall projections for vision system sales are, if anything, very conservative.

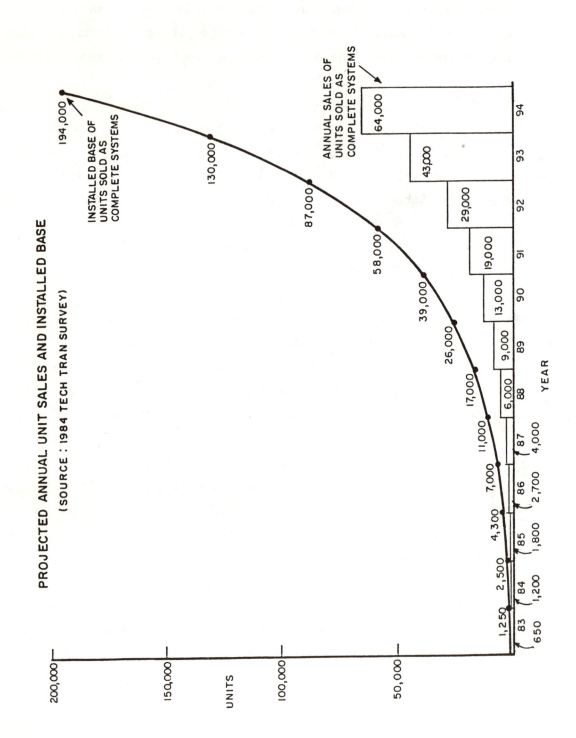

PROJECTED ANNUAL UNIT SALES AND INSTALLED BASE

(SOURCE : 1984 TECH TRAN SURVEY)

EXHIBIT 39

In terms of sales revenue, the 1984 market was about $58 million, according to the survey. This figure includes only the revenue generated from commercial sales of complete vision systems, and does not include component sales or revenue from other services, such as applications engineering. When these other sources of revenue are included, the total 1984 sales were around $87 million (see Exhibit 33).

Sales revenue is expected to increase from $58 million in 1984 to about $1,200 million in 1994, as shown in Exhibit 40. This represents a compound annual growth rate of about 35%. The lower growth rate when compared to unit sales is due to decreasing unit costs. Using this data, the average system price in 1984 was about $48,000. This average price should drop to around $19,000 by 1994. If you add in the revenue generated from component sales and other sources (assuming the ratio of sales remains the same as shown in Exhibit 33) then the total annual sales in 1994 would be approximately $1,800 million.

Although machine vision systems are being used by almost every manufacturing industry, and will continue to do so, past sales have been mainly to the automotive and electronics industries, as shown in Exhibit 41. Collectively, these two industries have accounted for about 60% of all units sold. By 1994, these two industries are expected to continue to dominate the market, with combined sales of slightly over 50%. The remainder of sales will be fairly evenly distributed among the other user industries.

Although the number of vision systems in use is expected to grow dramatically, the kinds of applications they will be used for will remain relatively unchanged, as shown in Exhibits 42 and 43. This is a somewhat surprising survey result since many observers felt there would be a major shift in types of applications from inspection to guidance and control. The only major change identified by the survey

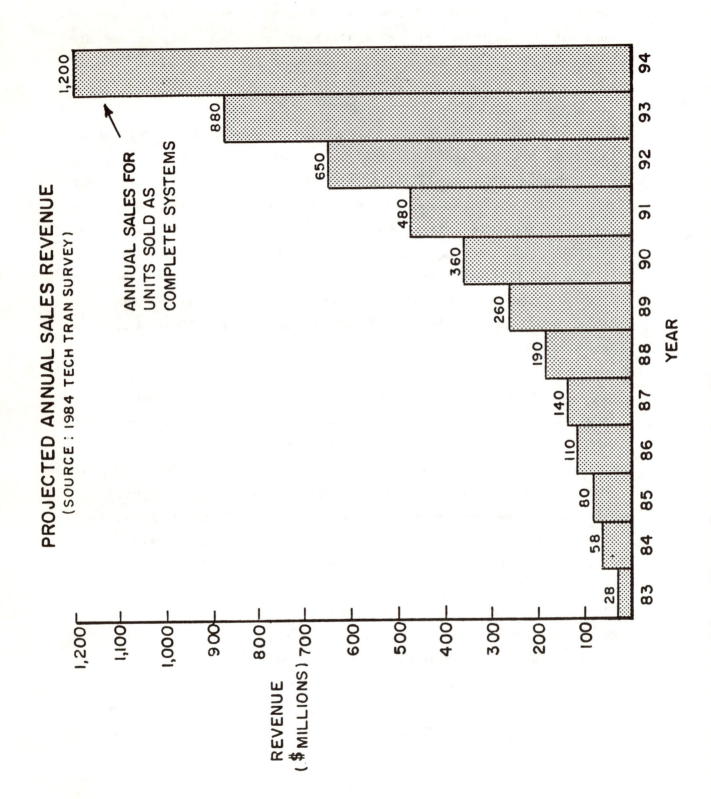

PROJECTED ANNUAL SALES REVENUE
(SOURCE: 1984 TECH TRAN SURVEY)

ANNUAL SALES FOR
UNITS SOLD AS
COMPLETE SYSTEMS

REVENUE
($ MILLIONS)

YEAR

EXHIBIT 40

EXHIBIT 41

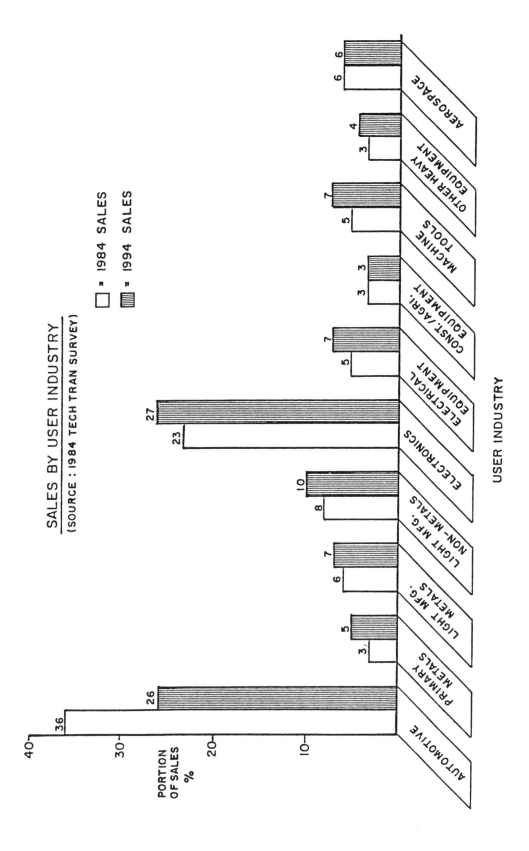

SALES BY USER INDUSTRY
(SOURCE : 1984 TECH TRAN SURVEY)

☐ = 1984 SALES
▤ = 1994 SALES

PORTION OF SALES %

USER INDUSTRY

EXHIBIT 42

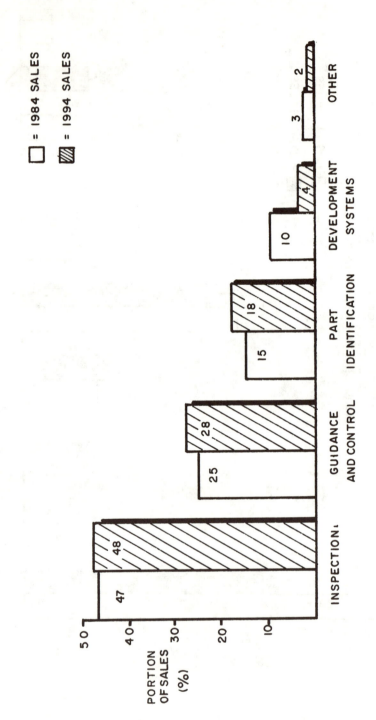

SYSTEM SALES BY TYPE OF APPLICATION
(SOURCE : 1984 TECH TRAN SURVEY)

☐ = 1984 SALES

▨ = 1994 SALES

EXHIBIT 43

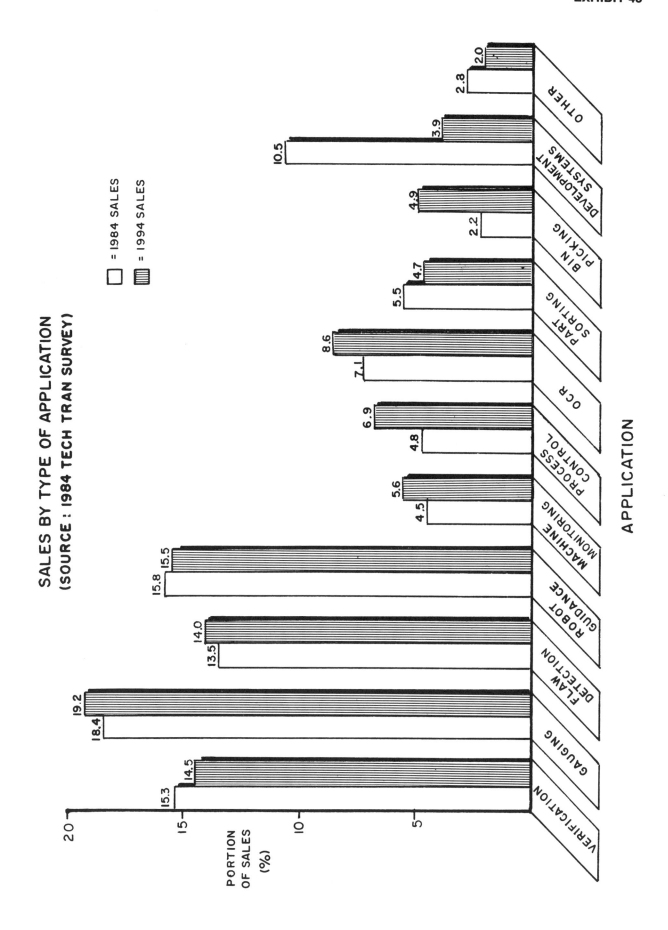

SALES BY TYPE OF APPLICATION
(SOURCE : 1984 TECH TRAN SURVEY)

□ = 1984 SALES
▤ = 1994 SALES

PORTION OF SALES (%)

APPLICATION

is a decline in the portion of sales that represent development systems, dropping from 10% in 1984 to only 4% by 1994.

In addition to changes in sales, user industries, and applications, several other important trends are affecting the industry. These trends are best viewed from the perspective of how the industry is evolving.

A number of individuals and consulting firms have developed models to describe and analyze the growth patterns and other characteristics of industries. These models generally view the life of an industry in roughly five phases: (1) industry definition; (2) initial growth; (3) consolidation and sustained growth; (4) maturity; and (5) decline.

During the industry definition phase, a few pioneering firms expend considerable resources to demonstrate the technology and its potential. This first phase may take five to ten years to complete.

The second phase, initial growth, takes place when potential users of the technology and the financial community, among others, becomes aware of and actively interested in the industry. This phase is usually accompanied by an influx of new start-up manufacturers and venture capital, as well as sales increases due in part to experimentation by users. However, at this stage of evolution, the industry is not yet large enough to support the number of suppliers, and financial losses are heavy. At the end of this phase, larger companies begin to view the industry as attractive and consequently they enter the market, placing even greater pressure on the collective financial resources of the industry.

During the third phase, consolidation and sustained growth, the industry undergoes a "shake out" and weak suppliers withdraw from the market. The industry continues to grow and a few manufacturers emerge as dominant forces in the industry.

Clearly, the machine vision industry is in the second phase, initial growth. Pioneers such as Machine Intelligence Company, Diffracto and View Engineering have been developing the market for a number of years, and a large number of firms have entered the market since the early 1980's. Large companies, such as Honeywell, Kodak and 3M have also joined the competition recently, and several others are likely to enter the market soon.

It is equally clear that the current market cannot sustain the number of manufacturers presently offering machine vision systems. An industry shake out is inevitable and, in fact, has already started. Which companies will emerge as the dominant suppliers is far from being determined at present. This type of change is good for the industry and usually results in better products and services for the end user.

Machine vision promises to be one of the more important technologies that will affect manufacturing during the next decade.

APPENDIX A
LIST OF VISION SYSTEM ORGANIZATIONS

<u>SYSTEM MANUFACTURERS</u>

Adaptive Technologies, Inc.
600 W. North Market Blvd., #1
Sacramento, CA   95834
916/920-9119

Adept Technology, Inc.
1212 Bordeaux Drive
Sunnyvale, CA   94089
408/747-0111

Advanced Robotics Corp.
777 Manor Park Dr.
Columbus, OH   43228
614/870-7778

American Robot
121 Industry Drive
Pittsburgh, PA   15275
412/787-3000

Analog Devices
3 Technology Way
Norwood, MA   02062
617/329-4700

Applied Intelligent Systems
110 Parkland Plaza
Ann Arbor, MI   48103
313/995-2035

Applied Scanning Technology
1988 Leghorn St.
Mountain View, CA   94043
415/967-4211

ASEA Robotics Inc.
16250 W. Glendale Dr.
New Berlin, WI   53151
414/875-3400

Autoflex Inc.
25880 Commerce Drive

Madison Heights, MI 48071
313/398-9911

Automatic Inspection Devices
One SeaGate
Toledo, OH 43666
419/247-5000

Automatic Vision
1300 Richard St.
Vancouver, BC V6B 3G6
CN

Automation Intelligence
1200 W. Colonial Dr.
Orlando, FL 32804-7194
800/237-7030

Automation Systems Inc.
1106 Federal Rd.
Brookfield, CT 06804
203/775-2581

Automatix
1000 Tech Park Dr.
Billerica, MA 01821
617/667-7900

Beeco Inc.
4175 Millersville Rd.
Indianapolis, IN 46205
317/547-1717

Cambridge Instruments Inc./
   Sub. Cambridge Instruments Ltd.
40 Robert Pitt Dr.
Monsey, NY 10952
914/356-3331 or 356-3877

CBIT Corporation
Horse Shoe Trail RD #2
Chester Springs, PA 19425
215/469-0358

Cochlea
2284 Ringwood Ave., Unit C
San Jose, CA 95131
408/942-8228

Cognex
72 River Park St.

Needham, MA 02194
617/449-6030

Computer Systems Co.
26401 Harper Ave.
St. Clair Shores, MI 48081
313/779-8700

Contrex
47 Manning Rd.
Billerica, MA 01821
617/273-3434

Control Automation
Princeton-Windsor Industrial Park
P. O. Box 2304
Princeton, NJ 08540
609/799-6026

COSMOS Imaging Systems, Inc.
30100 Crown Valley
  Parkway Suite 32
Laguna Niguel, CA 92677
714/495-2662

CR Technology
1701 Reynolds Ave.
Irvine, CA 92714
714/751-6901

Cybotech
P. O. Box 88514
Indianapolis, IN 46208
317/298-5890

DCI Corp.
110 S. Gold Dr.
Robbinsville, NJ 08691
609/587-9132

Diffracto, Ltd.
6360 Hawthorne Dr.
Windsor, Ontario N8T 1J9
Canada
519/945-6373

Digital/Analog Design Assoc.
530 Broadway
New York, NY 10012
212/966-0410

Eaton Corporation

4201 N. 27th St.
Milwaukee, WI 53216
414/449-6345

Eigen/Optivision
P.O. Box 848
Nevada City, CA 95959
916/272-3461

Electro-Optical Information Systems
710 Wilshire Blvd.
Suite 501
Santa Monica, CA 90401
213/451-8566

Everett/Charles Test
Equipment, Inc.
2887 N. Towne Ave.
Pomona, CA 91767
714/621-9511

Federal Products Corp.
Boice Division
P. O. Box 12-185
Albany, NY 12212
518/785-2211

Gallaher Enterprises
P. O. Box 10244
Winston-Salem, NC 27108-0318
919/725-8494

General Electric
P. O. Box 17500
Orlando, FL 32860-7500
305/889-1200

General Numeric Corp.
390 Kent Ave.
Elk Grove Village, IL 60007
312/640-1595

GMF Robotics Corp.
Northfield Hills Corp. Center
5600 New King St.
Troy, MI 48098
313/641-4242

Hamamatsu Systems
40 Bear Hill Rd.
Waltham, MA 02154
617/890-3440

Ham Industries
835 Highland Rd.
Macedonia, OH   44056
216/467-4256

Hitachi America, Ltd.
50 Prospect Ave.
Tarrytown, NY   10591-4698
914/332-5800

Honeywell Visitronics
P. O. Box 5077
Englewood, CO   80155
303/850-5050

Image Data Systems
315 W. Huron, Suite 140
Ann Arbor, MI   48103
313/761-7222

Industrial Technology and
  Machine Intelligence
1 Speen St., Suite 240
Framingham, MA   01701
617/620-0184

Industrial Vision Systems, Inc.
Victory Research Park
452 Chelmsford St.
Lowell, MA   01851
617/459-9000

Integrated Automation
2121 Allston Way
Berkeley, CA   94704
415/843-8227

Intelledex Inc.
33840 Eastgate Circle
Corvallis, OR   97333
503/758-4700

International Imaging Systems
1500 Buckeye Dr.
Milpitas, CA   95035
408/262-4444

International Robomation/
Intelligence
2281 Las Palmas Dr.
Carlsbad, CA   92008

619/438-4424

IRT Corp.
3030 Callan Rd.
P. O. Box 85317
San Diego, CA 92138-5317
619/450-4343

Itek Optical Systems/
Litton Industries
10 Maguire Rd.
Lexington, MA 02173
617/276-2000

ITRAN
670 N. Commercial St.
P. O. Box 607
Manchester, NH 03105
603/669-6332

Key Image Systems
20100 Plummer St.
Chatsworth, CA 91311
213/993-1911

KLA Instruments
2051 Mission College
Santa Clara, CA 95054
408/988-6100

L. N. K. Corp.
P. O. Box 1619
College Park, MD 20740
301/927-3223

Machine Intelligence Corp.
330 Potrero Ave.
Sunnyvale, CA 94086
408/737-7960

Machine Vision International
Burlington Center
325 E. Eisenhower
Ann Arbor, MI 48104
313/996-8033

Mack Corporation
3695 East Industrial Dr.
P. O. Box 1756
Flagstaff, AZ 86002
602/526-1120

Micro-Poise
P. O. Box 88512
Indianapolis, IN 46208
317/298-5000

Nikon Instrument Group
623 Stewart Ave.
Garden City, NY 11530
516/222-0200

Object Recognition Systems
1101-8 State Rd.
Princeton, NJ 08540
609/924-1667

Octek
7 Corporate Place
South Bedford St.
Burlington, MA 01803
617/273-0851

Opcon
720 80th St. S. W.
Everett, WA 98203
206/353-0900

Optical Gaging Products
850 Hudson Ave.
Rochester, NY 14621
716/544-0400

Optical Specialties
4281 Technology Drive
Fremont, CA 94538
415/490-6400

Optrotech Inc.
Suite 206
111 S. Bedford St.
Burlington, MA 01803
617/272-4050

Pattern Processing
Technologies
511 Eleventh Ave. S.
Minneapolis, MN 55415
612/339-8488

Penn Video
929 Sweitzer Ave.
Akron, OH 44311
216/762-4840

Perceptron
23855 Research Dr.
Farmington Hills, MI   48024
313/478-7710

Photonic Automation, Inc.
3633 W. McArthur Blvd.
Santa Ana, CA   92704
714/546-6651

Photo Research Vision Systems
Division of Kollmorgen
3099 N. Lima St.
Burbank, CA   91504
818/954-0104

Prothon
Div. of Video Tek
199 Pomeroy Rd.
Parsippany, NJ   07054
201/887-8211

Quantex Corp.
252 N. Wolfe Rd.
Sunnyvale, CA   94086
408/733-6730

Rank Videometrix
9421 Winnetka
Chatsworth, CA   91311
818/343-3120

Recognition Concepts Inc.
924 Incline Way
P. O. Box 8510
Incline Village, NV   89450
702/831-0473

Robotic Vision Systems
425 Rabro Dr. E.
Hauppauge, NY   11788
516/273-9700

Selcom
P. O. Box 250
Valdese, NC   28690
704/874-4102

SILMA, Inc.
1800 Embarcadero
Palo Alto, CA   94301

415/493-0145

Spatial Data Systems
420 S. Fairview Ave.
P. O. Box 978
Goleta, CA 93117
805/967-2383

Synthetic Vision Systems
2929 Plymouth Rd.
Ann Arbor, MI 48105
313/665-1850

Syn-Optics
1225 Elko Dr.
Sunnyvale, CA 94089
408/734-8563

Technical Arts Corp.
180 Nickerson St. #303
Seattle, WA 98109
206/282-1703

Testerion, Inc.
9645 Arrow Hwy.
P. O. Box 694
Cucamonga, CA 91730
714/987-0025

Time Engineering
1630 Big Beaver Rd.
Troy, MI 48083
313/528-9000

Unimation
Shelter Rock Lane
Danbury, CT 06810
203/744-1800

United Detector Technology
12525 Chadron Ave.
Hawthorne, CA 90250
213/978-0516

Vektronics
5750 El Camino Real
P.O. Box 459
Carlsbad, CA 92008
619/438-0992

Vicom Systems
2520 Junction Ave.

San Jose, CA 95134
408/946-5660

Videk
Division of Eastman Technology
343 State St.
Rochester, NY 14650
800/445-6325 Ext. 15

View Engineering
1650 N. Voyager Ave.
Simi Valley, CA 93063
805/522-8439

Visionetics
P. O. Box 189
Brookfield Center, CT 06805
203/775-4770

Vision System Technologies
1532 S. Washington Ave.
Piscataway, NJ 08854
201/752-6700

Visual Matic
2171 El Camino Real
Oceanside, CA 92054
619/722-8299

Vuebotics Corp.
6086 Corte Del Cedro
Carlsbad, CA 92008
619/438-7994

3M, Vision Systems
Suite 300
8301 Greensboro Dr.
McLean, VA 22102
703/734-0300

CAMERA MANUFACTURERS

AFP Imaging
Video Products Group
50 Executive Blvd.
Elmsford, NY 10523
914/592-6100

Artek Systems

170 Finn Court
Farmingdale, NY 11735
516/293-4420

Circon
749 Wood Dr.
Santa Barbara, CA 93111
805/967-0404

Cohu Inc./Electronics Div.
5725 Kearny Villa Rd.
Box 85623
San Diego, CA 92138
619/277-6700

Cyberanimation, Inc.
4621 Granger Rd.
Akron, OH 44313
216/666-8293

Cybergen Systems Corp.
2070 Walsh Ave.
Santa Clara, CA 95050
408/727-6766

Datacopy Corp.
1215 Terra Bella
Mountain View, CA 94043
415/965-7900

EG&G Reticon
345 Potrero Ave.
Sunnyvale, CA 94086
408/738-4266

Eikonix
23 Crosby Dr.
Bedford, MA 01730
617/275-5070

Fairchild CCD Imaging
3440 Hillview Ave.
Palo Alto, CA 94304
415/493-8001

General Electric Co.
Electronic Camera Operation
890 7th North St.
Liverpool, NY 13088
315/456-2834

ITT

Electro-Optical Products Div.
3700 E. Pontiac St.
Fort Wayne, IN 46801
219/423-4341

Javelin Electronics
19831 Magellan Dr.
P. O. Box 2033
Torrance, CA 90502
213/327-7440

Micron Technology, Inc.
2805 E. Columbia Rd.
Boise, ID 83706
208/383-4000

MII
P. O. Box 395
Birdsboro, PA 19508
215/562-5361

Optron Corp.
30 Hazel Terrace
Woodbridge, CT 06525
203/389-5384

Panasonic Industrial Company
Electronic Components Division
One Panasonic Way
Secaucus, NJ 07094
201/348-5277

Periphicon
P. O. Box 324
Beaverton, OR 97075
503/222-4966

Pulnix America, Inc.
453 Ravendale Dr.
Mountain View, CA 94043
415/964-0955

RCA
Closed-Circuit Video Equip.
New Holland Ave.
Lancaster, PA 17604
717/397-7661

Sierra Scientific
2598 Bayshore Frontage Rd.
Mountain View, CA 94043
415/969-9315

Sony Corporation of America
15 Essex Rd.
Paramus, NJ 07652
201/368-5000

Thomson - CSF
Components Corp.
Electron Tube Div.
301 Route 17 North
Rutherford, NJ 07070
201/438-2300

Video Logic Corp.
597 N. Mathilda Ave.
Sunnyvale, CA 94086
408/245-8622

Video Measurements
10 Havens St.
Elmsford, NY 10523
914/592-2025

VSP Labs
670 Airport Blvd.
Ann Arbor, MI 48104
313/769-5522

Xybion Electronic Systems
7750-A Convoy Ct.
San Diego, CA 92111
619/277-8220

COMPONENT MANUFACTURERS

American Volpi
26 Aurelius Ave.
Auburn, NY 13021
315/255-1105

Chorus Data Systems
P.O. Box 810
27 Proctor Hill Rd.
Hollis, NH 03049
603/465-7100

Colorado Video Inc.
P.O. Box 928
Boulder, CO 80306

303/444-3972

Datacube
4 Dearborn Rd.
Peabody, MA 01960
617/535-6644

Data-Sud Systems/U. S.
2219 S. 48th St.
Suite J
Tempe, AZ 85282
602/438-1492

Digital Graphics Systems
2629 Terminal Bl.
Mountain View, CA 94043
415/962-0200

Dolan-Jenner Industries
Blueberry Hill Industrial Park
P. O. Box 1020
Woburn, MA 01801-0820
617/935-7444

General Scanning
500 Arsenal St.
P. O. Box 307
Watertown, MA 02172
617/924-1010

Imaging Technology
600 W. Cummings Park
Woburn, MA 01801
617/938-8444

I.T.M.I.
1 Speen St., Suite 240
Framingham, MA 01701
617/576-2585

Microtex
80 Trowbridge St.
Cambridge, MA 02138
617/491-2874

Poynting Products, Inc.
P. O. Box 1227
Oak Park, IL 60304
312/489-6638

Toko America, Inc.
5520 W. Touhy Ave.

Skokie, IL 60077
312/677-3640

Videtics Ltd.
258 King St. N.
Waterloo, Ontario N2J 2Y9
Canada
519/885-6852

CONSULTANTS AND SYSTEM INTEGRATORS

Anorad Corp.
110 Oser Ave.
Hauppauge, NY 11788
516/231-1990

Automated Vision Systems
1590 La Pradera Dr.
Campbell, CA 95008
408/370-0229

Automation Unlimited
10 Roessler Rd.
Woburn, MA 01801
617/933-7288

Bahr Technologies Inc.
1842 Hoffman St.
Madison, WI 53704
608/244-0500

Hansford Manufacturing
3111 Winton Road South
Rochester, NY 14623
716/427-8150

Image Technology Methods Corp.
103 Moody St.
Waltham, MA 02154
617/894-1720

Key Technology Inc.
517 N. Elizabeth
P. O. Box 8
Milton-Freewater, OR 97862

Medar, Inc.
38700 Grand River Ave.

Farmington Hills, MI   48018
313/477-3900

Multicon
7035 Main St.
Cincinnati, OH   45244
513/271-0200

Raycon Corp.
77 Enterprise
Ann Arbor, MI   48103
313/769-2614

Robotic Objectives, Inc.
60 Church St., The Forum
Yalesville, CT   06492
203/269-5063

Spectron Engineering
800 W. 9th Ave.
Denver, CO   80204
303/623-8987

TAU Corp.
10 Jackson St., Ste. 101
Los Gatos, CA   95030
408/395-9191

Tech Tran Corporation
134 N. Washington St.
Naperville, IL 60540
312/369-9232

Vision Systems International
3 Milton Dr.
Yardley, PA   19067
215/736-0994

Visual Intelligence Corp.
Amherst Fields Research Park
160 Old Farm Road
Amherst, MA   01002
413/253-3482

RESEARCH ORGANIZATIONS

Carnegie-Mellon University
The Robotics Institute
Pittsburgh, PA   15213
412/578-3826

Environmental Research Institute of Michigan
Robotics Program
P. O. Box 8618
Ann Arbor, MI 48107
313/994-1200

George Washington University
725 23rd Street, N.W.
Washington, DC 20052
202/676-6919

Jet Propulsion Labs
Robotics Group
4800 Oak Grove Drive
Pasadena, CA 91103
213/354-6101

Massachusetts Institute of Technology
Artificial Intelligence Lab
545 Technology Square
Cambridge, MA 02139
617/253-6218

National Bureau of Standards
Industrial Systems Division
Building 220, Room A123
Washington, DC 20234
301/921-2381

Naval Research Lab
Code 2610
Washington, DC 20375
202/767-3984

North Carolina State University
Department of Electrical Engineering
Raleigh, NC 27650
919/737-2376

Purdue University
School of Electrical Engineering
West Lafayette, IN 47906
317/749-2607

Rensselaer Polytechnic Institute
Center for Manufacturing Productivity
Jonsson Engineering Center
Troy, NY 12181
518/270-6724

SRI International
Artificial Intelligence Center

Menlo Park, CA   94025
425/497-2797

Stanford University
Artificial Intelligence Lab
Stanford, CA   94022
415/497-2797

U. S. Air Force
AFWAL/MLTC
Wright Patterson AFB, OH 45437
513/255-6976

University of Central Florida
IEMS Department
Orlando, FL   32816
305/275-2236

University of Cincinnati
Institute of Applied Interdisciplinary
Research
Location 42
Cincinnati, OH   45221
513/475-6131

University of Maryland
Computer Vision Laboratory
College Park, MD   20742
301/454-4526

University of Rhode Island
Department of Electrical Engineering
Kingston, RI   02881
401/792-2187

University of Southern California
School of Engineering
University Park
Los Angeles, CA

University of Texas
Austin, TX   78712
512/471-1331

University of Washington
Department of Electrical Engineering
Seattle, WA   98195
206/543-2056

APPENDIX B
RECOMMENDED MACHINE VISION
PUBLISHED INFORMATION SOURCES

BOOKS

Aleksander, I., "Artificial Vision for Robots," Chapman and Hall, 1983.*

Ballard, D. H. and C. M. Brown, "Computer Vision," Prentice-Hall, 1982.*

Baxes, G. A., "Digital Image Processing," Prentice-Hall, 1984.*

Brady, J. M., "Computer Vision," North-Holland, 1981.*

Castleman, K. R., "Digital Image Processing," Prentice-Hall, 1979.*

Dodd, G. G. and L. Rossol, "Computer Vision and Sensor-Based Robots," Plenum, 1979.*

Faugeras, O., "Fundamentals in Computer Vision," Cambridge University, 1983.*

Fu, K., "VLSI for Pattern Recognition and Image Processing," Springer-Verlag, 1984.*

Geverter, W. B., "An Overview of Computer Vision," U. S. Department of Commerce, 1982.*

Gomersall, A., "Machine Intelligence: An International Bibliography with Abstracts on Sensors in Automated Manufacturing," Springer-Verlag, 1984.*

Goos, G. and J. Hartmanis, "Digital Image Processing Systems," Springer-Verlag, 1981.*

Hollingum, J., "Machine Vision: The Eyes of Automation," Springer-Verlag, 1984.*

Onoe, M., et al, "Real-Time/Parallel Computing: Image Analysis." Plenum, 1981.*

Pao, Y. H. and G. W. Ernst, "Context-Directed Pattern Recognition and Machine Intelligence Techniques for Information Processing," IEEE, 1982.

---

* - Available from: The Manufacturing Technology Bookstore™, P.O. Box 206, Lake Geneva, Wisconsin 53147 (414/248-2200)

Pratt, W. K., "Digital Image Processing," John Wiley, 1978.*

Pugh, A., "Robot Vision," Springer-Verlag, 1983.*

Stucki, P., "Advances in Digital Image Processing," Plenum, 1979.*

_____, "Machine Vision," Society of Manufacturing Engineers, 1984.*

CONFERENCE PROCEEDINGS

Brady, M. and R. Paul, "Robotics Research: The First International Symposium," MIT Press, 1984.*

Rosenfeld, A., "Proc. of SPIE Conference on Robot Vision," SPIE, 1982.

Casasent, D. P., "Proc. of SPIE Conference on Robotics and Industrial Inspection," SPIE, 1982.

_____, "The Third Annual Applied Machine Vision Conference Proceedings," Robotics International of SME, 1984.*

_____, "Proc. of Conference on Industrial Applications of Machine Vision," IEEE, 1982.

_____, "Proc. of Conference on Pattern Recognition and Image Processing," IEEE, 1981.

_____, "Robotics Research: The Next Five Years and Beyond," Robotics International of SME, 1984.*

_____, "Robots 8 Conference Proceedings," SME, 1984.*

_____, "Proc. of 1st International Conference on Robot Vision and Sensory Control," IFS (Publications), 1981.

_____, "Proc. of 2nd International Conference on Robot Vision and Sensory Controls," IFS (Publications), 1982.

_____, "Proc. of the 3rd International Conference on Robot Vision and Sensory Controls," North-Holland, 1983.*

_____

* - Available from: The Manufacturing Technology Bookstore™, P.O. Box 206, Lake Geneva, Wisconsin 53147 (414/248-2200)

RELATED PERIODICALS

Electronic Imaging
Morgan-Grampian Publishing Co.
Berkshire Common
Pittsfield, Massachusetts 01201
(413) 499-2550

Image and Vision Computing
Butterworth Scientific Ltd.
P. O. Box 63
Westbury House, Bury St.
Guildford, Surrey GU1 5BH
United Kingdom

Manufacturing Technology Horizons
Tech Tran Corporation
134 N. Washington Street
Naperville, Illinois 60540
(312) 369-9232

Photonics Spectra
Optical Publishing Co. Inc.
P. O. Box 1146
Berkshire Common
Pittsfield, Massachusetts 01202
(413) 499-0514

Robotics Technology Abstracts
Tech Tran Corporation
134 N. Washington Street
Naperville, Illinois 60540
(312) 369-9232

Robotics Today
Society of Manufacturing Engineers
One SME Drive
P. O. Box 930
Dearborn, Michigan 48128
(313) 271-1500

Sensors
North American Technology, Inc.
174 Concord Street
Peterborough, New Hampshire 03458
(603) 924-7261

The International Journal or
 Robotics Research
MIT Press
28 Carleton Street
Cambridge, Massachusetts 02142
(617) 253-2889

Vision
Society of Manufacturing Engineers
One SME Drive
P. O. Box 930
Dearborn, Michigan 48128
(313) 271-1500

APPENDIX C
SELECTED GLOSSARY OF MACHINE VISION TERMS

ACCURACY - The extent to which a machine vision system can correctly interpret an image, generally expressed as a percentage to reflect the likelihood of a correct interpretation.

AMBIENT LIGHT - Light which is present in the environment around a machine vision system and generated from outside sources. This light must be treated as background noise by the vision system.

AMBIGUITY - The characteristic of an image in which more than one interpretation of the object from which the image was formed can be made. There is no ambiguity when only one interpretation is possible.

ANALOG - The representation of data as a smooth, continuous function.

ANALOG/DIGITAL CONVERTER - A device which converts an analog voltage signal to a digital signal for computer processing.

ARTIFICIAL INTELLIGENCE - The ability of a machine to perform certain complex functions normally associated with human intelligence, such as judgment, pattern recognition, understanding, learning, planning, and problem solving.

BACK LIGHTING - The use of a light source placed behind an object so that a clear silhouette of an object is formed. This is used when surface features on an object are not important.

BINARY SYSTEM - A vision system which creates a digitized image of an object in which each pixel can have one of only two values, such as black/white, or one/zero.

BOUNDARY - The line formed by the joining of two image regions, each having a different light intensity.

CCD (CHARGE-COUPLED DEVICE) CAMERA - A solid-state camera which uses a self-scanning semiconductor imaging device placed on a silicon array to transform light into a digitized image. The device reads pixel brightnesses using a line-by-line scan pattern.

CID (CHARGE-INJECTION DEVICE) CAMERA - A solid-state camera which forms a digitized image through the use of a device consisting of an array of metallic electrodes. Each electrode creates one pixel of the image by generating a flow of electrical current proportional to the image brightness at that point. Pixels can then be read out in an arbitrary sequence, unlike CCD cameras, which follow a line pattern.

COMPUTER VISION - See machine vision.

CONTRAST - The difference in light intensities between two regions in an image. This term is generally used to measure the difference between the lightest and darkest portion of an image.

CONTROLLER - An information processing device which receives inputs from the vision system in the form of image interpretation data and then converts this data into command signals for robots or other equipment.

DEPTH PERCEPTION - The ability to perceive differences in distance from an observer to one point relative to the distance to another point.

DETECTOR - A device which converts light into electrical signals.

DIGITAL - The representation of data as discrete points. The process of digitzing an image converts analog light into an array of digital elements, each with a discrete value.

DISCRIMINATION - The degree to which a vision system is capable of sensing differences in light intensity between two regions.

EDGE - The apparent termination of an object's image. For a curved object such as a sphere, an edge represents the perimeter of the image formed by a series of lines from the observer and tangent to the surface of the object. An edge represents the outer boundary of an image.

ENCODER - See optical encoder.

FEATURE - An optical characteristic of an image which describes it in such a way that an interpretation can be made of the object which formed the image. Features may include position, geometric characteristics or light intensity distribution over the image.

FIBER OPTICS - A light source for vision systems by which light is transmitted through a long flexible fiber of transparent material through a series of internal reflections.

FIELD OF VIEW - The maximum angle of view which can be seen through a camera. As an object moves closer to the camera, the angle does not change, but a smaller portion of the object is seen by the camera.

FIXTURE - A device to hold and locate a workpiece during processing or inspection operations.

FLEXIBLE MANUFACTURING SYSTEM - An arrangement of machines, such as NC machining centers and robots, interconnected by a transport system and under the control of a central computer.

FOURIER PROCESSING - A mathematical method of representing an image as a series of superimposed sinusoidal functions.

FRAME - A single image at a specific point in time, stored for processing and analysis by a computer.

FRONT LIGHTING - The use of illumination in front of an object so that surface features can be observed.

GEOMETRIC CONFIGURATION - The group of features which describe the shape of an image, such as area, centroid, perimeter, dimensions, etc.

GRAY SCALE IMAGE - An image consisting of an array of pixels which can have more than two values. Typically, up to sixteen levels are possible for each pixel.

HIERARCHICAL CONTROL - A control technique in which processes are arranged in a hierarchy according to priority.

ILLUMINATION - The use of a light source to generate a light intensity distribution based upon the way in which light is reflected from an object's surface.

IMAGE - A two-dimensional representation of an object or a scene formed by creating a pattern from the light received from the scene.

IMAGE ENHANCEMENT - The use of processing techniques to improve the nature of the information received from an image.

IMAGE PROCESSOR - A device such as a microprocessor which converts an image to digital form and then further enhances the image to prepare it in a form suitable for computer analysis.

INTENSITY - The relative brightness of an image or portion of an image.

INTERFACE - A shared boundary, such as a mechanical or electrical connection between two devices. Another example is a portion of computer storage which is accessed by two or more programs.

JIG - A device which holds and locates a workpiece at the same time it guides, controls, or limits a cutting tool.

LIGHT PEN - A hand-held, light sensitive device used to provide instructions to a vision system directly through a display console. The pen touches a specific area on the monitor screen, and commands are transmitted to a computer.

LINEAR ARRAY - A solid-state video detector consisting of a single row of light sensitive semiconductor devices. This is used in linear array cameras.

LOCATION - The coordinates of an image or object relative to an observer. An image location is defined by the X-Y coordinates of its centroid. A three-dimensional object's location is defined by the X, Y, and Z coordinates of some point, such as its center of gravity.

MACHINE VISION - The ability of an automated system to perform certain visual tasks normally associated with human vision, including sensing, image formation, image analysis, and image interpretation or decision making.

MASKING - The process of creating an outline around a standard image and then comparing this outline with test images to determine how closely they match.

MATRIX ARRAY CAMERA - A solid-state camera which forms an MxN array of pixels when generating an image.

MONITOR - A closed circuit television system that allows the vision system operator to view the image of the object being investigated.

MOTION SENSING - The ability of a vision system to: (1) form an mage of an object which is in motion, and (2) to determine the direction and speed of that motion.

NTSC (NATIONAL TELEVISION SYSTEM COMMITTEE) STANDARD - Standard used for television signals in the United States in which a full TV Picture frame is composed of 525 scan lines interlaced into two fields of 262.5 lines at a rate of 30 frames per record.

OBJECT - A three-dimensional figure or shape which is the subject of investigation for a vision system. An object forms the basis for creating an image.

OCCLUSION - The inability to see a portion of an object because an obstruction has been placed between the object and the observer.

OPTICAL CHARACTER RECOGNITION - The ability of a vision system to identify an alphanumeric character.

OPTICAL COMPARATOR - A gaging device which accurately measures dimensions of objects using back lighting. This device does not analyze the image or make decisions.

OPTICAL ENCODER - A device which measures linear or rotary motion by detecting the movement of markings past a fixed beam of light.

ORIENTATION - The angle formed by the major axis of an image relative to a reference axis. For an object, the direction of the major axis must be defined relative to a three-dimensional coordinate system.

PARALLAX - The change in perspective of an object when viewed from two slightly different positions. The object appears to shift position relative to its background, and it also appears to rotate slightly.

PARALLEL PROCESSING - The processing of pixel data in such a way that a group of pixels are analyzed at one time rather than one pixel at a time.

PATTERN RECOGNITION - The process of identifying an object based upon an analysis of several features of the object's image.

PIXEL - A small element of a scene, or "picture element", in which an average brightness value is determined and used to represent that portion of the scene. Pixels are arranged in a rectangular array to form a complete image of the scene.

POSITION - The definition of an object's location in space, its orientation, and its velocity.

PROCESSING SPEED - The time required for a vision system to analyze and interpret an image. Typical vision systems can inspect from two to fifteen parts per second.

RANGE SENSING - The measurement of distance to an object.

REAL TIME PROCESSING - The ability of a vision system to interpret an image in a short enough time to keep pace with most manufacturing operations.

REGION - An area of an image over which the light intensity is constant. A region ends when it meets another region with a different intensity level. Regions are formed by such object characteristics as flat surfaces, areas of constant colors, or shadows.

RESOLUTON - The smallest feature of an image which can be sensed by a vision system. Resolution is generally a function of the number of pixels in the image, with a greater number of pixels allowing better resolution.

RELIABILITY - See accuracy. In this context, reliability is distinguished from the frequency of failure of the system.

ROBOT VISION - The use of a vision system to provide visual feedback to an industrial robot. Based upon the vision system's interpretation of a scene, the robot may be commanded to move in a certain way.

SCENE - The portion of space being investigated by a vision system. A scene may be very complex, or it may consist simply of a single item.

SEGMENTATION - The process of dividing a scene into a number of individually defined regions, or segments. Each segment can then be analyzed separately.

SHADING - The variation of relative illumination over the surface of an object caused, for example, by curvature of the surface.

SOLID-STATE CAMERA - A camera which uses a solid-state integrated circuit to convert light into an electrical signal.

STADIMETRY - The determination of distance based upon the apparent size of an object in the camera's field of view.

STEREOPSIS - The determination of distance through the use of binocular vision.

STROBE LIGHT - An electronic flash tube which produces hundreds or thousands of flashes of light per second. It is used to freeze images of moving objects for vision systems.

STRUCTURED LIGHT - The determination of three-dimensional characteristics of an object from the observed deflections that result when a plane or grid pattern of light is projected onto the object.

SURFACE - The visible outside portion of a solid object.

TEMPLATE MATCHING - The technique of comparing the image of a test object with that of a standard on a pixel-by-pixel basis for inspection or recognition purposes.

TEXTURE - The degree of smoothness of the surface of an object. The texture of an object's surface can affect the way in which light is reflected from it, and therefore the image brightness can be affected.

THRESHOLDING - The process of defining a specific intensity level for determining which of two values will be assigned to each pixel in binary processing. If the pixel's brightness is above the threshold level, it will appear white in the image. If the brightness is below the threshold level, it will appear black.

TRIANGULATION - A method of determining distance by forming a right triangle consisting of a light source, camera, and sample. Distance can be calculated if the distance between the camera and light source is known along with the angle between the incident and reflected light beam.

VERTICE - The intersection of two surfaces of an object.

VIDICON - A generic name for a TV camera tube often used in small cameras originally developed for use in closed circuit TV monitoring. It provides an analog voltage output corresponding to the intensity of the incoming light.

WINDOWING - A technique for reducing data processing requirements by electronically defining only a small portion of the image to be analyzed. All other parts of the image are ignored.